INVESTMENT CLUBS

ISBN: 978-198-099-635-4

ACKNOWLEDGEMENTS

I dedicate this book to the ONE,
thank you for birthing this idea and
helping me see it to this point.

To Deep, thank you for always being my sounding board
and always being so supportive, it means everything

To my children, you're the reason why this is important.

To my parents and siblings, thank you for your support.

To the members of my investment club,
thank you for starting this journey with me

And finally, to all those who helped review,
fine-tune and give feedback, thank you;

*Yvonne Yoyetakin, Mrs. Udo Okonjo, Rayo, Olaitan,
Toyin A, Toyin Ldr, Mrs. Sola Adesakin, Folakemi,
Nnnena, Chinedu, Segun K, Tola A, Nana, Ife, Isioma,
Jide, David, Nono Emah, Seyi Olufikayo, Femi A,
Lara Ojo, Alex.*

CONTENT

PART 1 - HOW TO START YOUR INVESTMENT CLUB

PART 2 - HOW TO MANAGE YOUR INVESTMENT CLUB

Group Effort, Not Individual Effort

PART 3 - HOW TO INVEST IN YOUR INVESTMENT CLUB

This Is What We Came to Do

Build Bridges, Not Walls

APPENDIX

Praise For The Book

Being an investor is one of the greatest ways to make the world a better place. Tomie has been running investment clubs for half a decade in Lagos, Nigeria one of the most dynamic ecosystems on the planet! This book does an amazing job in helping you understand exactly how this approach to working together yields better returns for each member of an investment club.
- *Tomi Davies, Founding President, African Business Angel Network*

This book is a great read. I like that it's to the point, with many useful points for those serious about building a sustainable investment club. For a beginner's guide and toolkit (and even for advanced clubs),
this book packs plenty of punches and will definitely be a useful guide for a lot of pooled investment groups.
- *Mrs Udo Okonjo, CEO & Vice Chairman, Fine & Country West Africa*

Tomie outlines, from her experience, the benefits of imbibing a savings/investing culture very early in one's working career as a means of growing financial wealth. I particularly like the contemporary chatty writing style of the book and will gladly recommend it to everyone who is new to investing especially entry -level employees or those already employed and/or wondering how to grow their financial wealth.
- *Sade Odunaiya, Founding President, Chartered Financial Analyst (CFA) Society, Nigeria*

This amazing book is a timely compendium of wisdom on everything to know about Investments and Investment Clubs. I believe it addresses the concerns and questions of the layman and even finance professionals regarding Investments.

Tomie has generously shared her experiences, successes and setbacks in driving home the points. Her style of writing is very enthralling, and

captivating and she has intricately blended her personal experiences with academic knowledge and technical competence to produce a masterwork. As a Personal Finance Expert, I ABSOLUTELY recommend this game-changing book!
- Mrs. Sola Adesakin CPA FCA FCCA MBA

This book is the real deal! It's an easy, interesting and very practical guide to creating wealth in an accelerated way. It doesn't teach you about money doubling schemes, instead it teaches you how to multiply wealth in even larger proportions.

Just as the African proverbs says, 'if you want to go fast, go alone; if you want to go far, go together', Tomie, in this book, teaches us how to go farther together on the wealth creation journey and she does it in the most easy-to-understand way. This book will not give you a headache, but it will make your eyes pop, expand your mind and get your hands taking notes furiously. The best part is that Tomie has included all the resources (worksheets, templates etc) that you need to start practicing all you learn from the book.

This book, the author and all the contents herein come highly recommended - I am a living witness to the power of investment clubs as taught by Tomie Balogun.
- *Kemi Onabanjo, Engagement Manager, Mckinsey & Company*

A Personal Message

I decided to write this book as a clear and in-depth guide expanding on answers to the frequent emails and direct messages asking how to start and manage an investment club. When I realized I was often repeating the same answers, I knew it was time to put a book together. That way, whenever anyone asked about investment clubs, I could refer them to one detailed source that held my knowledge on the subject.

When I started putting my thoughts together, based on my experience starting and operating an investment club for 4+ years, I assumed it would be a simple process. I was wrong.

Writing took me on a journey into understanding why I started an investment club with my friends, why we made good investment decisions, why we made some mistakes we made and lost money, why we have disagreements, and why we have remained a team despite all we have been through.

Digging deep to get the answers to these questions brought me to a key conclusion: An investment club is not a get-rich-quick fix. It is a long term, deliberate decision to build a sustainable investment portfolio.

If you start or join an investment club for the wrong reasons, you may not stick with it too long. Being a member of an investment club involves submitting to a process of gaining financial education, acting on that education, and seeing the results of your decisions—good or bad.

Becoming a member of an investment club remains a life changing experience for me. I have learnt a lot about myself and the other members of my club, in relation to money, discipline threshold, integrity, and risk tolerance. It is an experience I would not trade for anything.

This book begins with my journey on gaining clarity. I received my admission letter to the Lagos Business School MBA program and it dawned on me that I was broke. I knew my money habits had to change and thankfully I found a group of people who shared the same thoughts and we started an investment club together.

This book also shares the roadmap on how to start, manage, invest and grow your investment club based on my personal experience running one and working with over a dozen other clubs as they got started.

This book should be of interest to you whether or not you have invested before. It explains in very simple terms how you can create wealth beyond your pay-cheque by collaborating with people in your existing social or professional network.

The first time you read this book, you might only gain head (theoretical) knowledge; however, once you start your investment club, you will keep referring to it as the guide it is designed to be. So, my simple advice to you is: keep this book safe.

A few quick words on how to succeed with your investment club

Achieving success in your investment club will depend on how much the members want and are willing to work for it. Each member's commitment to the club's goals should take precedence over disagreements or relationship issues that might occur while managing and growing the investment club.

It will be a process—one that requires the patience and open-mindedness from all the members of the club. Please, trust the process.

As with all things, you must start. That is the first step towards success. But can I guarantee your success? No. That's up to all the members of your investment club. Will you achieve your investment goals sooner than if you had invested all by yourself? Most likely. Will you make mistakes? Will you lose money? Maybe and, honestly, that may not be a bad thing. When you make mistakes, learn what you can from it and just keep going. Yesterday's experiences give us the capacity to seize tomorrow's opportunities.

Also, please note that some concepts outlined in this book may differ based on your country of origin or residence.

You are advised to check for the specific application or otherwise of these concepts in your country of origin or residence or investment.

All the best on your investment journey and keep spreading the light.

Tomie Balogun, CFEI

FOREWORD

Being an investor is one of the greatest ways to make the world a better place. Bringing an entrepreneur's dream of building a company to life unlocks human potential and allows you to have enormous impact on your immediate and extended ecosystem.

I started my life as an angel investor in 2001 when I invested in Strika Entertainment, South African - creators of the animated series, SupaStrikas, which attracts millions of viewers in multiple languages on YouTube. The comic book we started with is now distributed in over a dozen countries. It is the first animated media property from Africa broadcast by Disney.

Since then, building my tech-centric portfolio of eight (and counting) early stage companies as an angel investor has been a fascinating learning journey full of dreams, plans, hopes, disappointments, achievements, and surprises. I have been fortunate, since we started the Lagos Angel Network (LAN) in 2012, to get the opportunity to share my lessons with members of the network.

Our continent Africa and country Nigeria are rich in a culture of savings manifest in schemes such as 'Ajo' and 'Esusu', and entrepreneurial apprenticeship evidenced by the 'Imu Olu'. Group-based investing, through Syndicates, Clubs, and Angel Networks, is therefore a natural alignment with our commercial psyche as a people. Done right, they hold the promise of 'Africans developing Africa' for us.

An investment club consolidates a group's funds for investment in deals and business opportunities, sharing both risks and rewards in a way that contributes to the growth of common wealth in society, while offering everyone—including those with limited funds—an opportunity to take advantage of its pooled funds for a win/win solution. Being part of an investment club enables you to invest the right way with a diverse team and leadership with defined roles and responsibilities, all working towards a common goal using a principle that Tomie shares as:

"Success = Your Assets + Other People's Assets"

This book does an amazing job of helping you to understand exactly how this approach to working together yields better returns for each co-investing member of the club.

What Tomie has done with her experience in setting up and running various investment club formats, is to provide a ready-to-use guide for those who have worked hard at putting away disposable income into savings and other cash-based instruments, and now want to put the money to work.

Once you've decided an investment club is for your group, the book builds on Tomie's personal experience, with expertise drawn from numerous sources, to present an investment club framework for reference and provide practical advice on how to go about setting up and running an investment club from a selection of club models, through to starting, managing, investing in, and growing the club while ensuring member goals are aligned.

Tomie has been running investment clubs for half a decade in Lagos, Nigeria, one of the most dynamic ecosystems on the planet! I can't say strongly enough how much I believe following the guidelines she has laid out here will help you build a worthwhile investment club.

H. Tomi Davies
Founding President, African Business Angel Network (ABAN)

March 2018

1
GAINING CLARITY

"Many people think investing is an exciting process,
where there is a lot of drama.
To me, Investing is a plan, often a dull, boring
and almost mechanical process of getting rich."
- Robert Kiyosaki

In 2011, my financial reality struck, and it hurt. I had no significant savings. I had not done any substantial investing over the course of 4+ years working in a boutique management consulting firm. Buried in regret, I looked back at years of work as images of all my careless spending on bags, shoes, and other depreciating assets flashed through my mind.

I had just received my admission to the MBA program of the Lagos Business School[1] and it was clear I needed to do things differently. I needed a lifeline, so I grabbed the

MBA as an opportunity to take a break and start afresh. With a firm resolve to get better at managing my money, I tendered my resignation at work and went on an exhilarating adventure to get my MBA. This journey proved worthwhile. There, I met and interacted with great classmates, some of who became my investment partners.

The 2-year MBA journey was not all fun and adventure. An MBA program can be a tough experience encompassing reading through pages of multiple case studies, working with groups of Type A students, and trying to hold your fort when questioned by inquisitive facilitators. In the beginning, it was a tough hill to climb, but working with smart classmates eased the stress a great deal.

Towards the end of my MBA program, I remembered my resolve to get better at managing my money, and I decided to act. I knew I had 'lost time' so I needed some sort of collaboration to redeem the time and resources I had lost whilst working and spending all the money I earned. In some discussions with a few classmates, the idea of pooling resources and investing came up, and I thought it was fantastic.

We decided to start immediately we each earned the first pay-cheque after the program. We agreed to pool resources and invest; however, we didn't call it an investment club until much later. All we knew was, it was a step higher than the traditional saving schemes. Known as the Ajo[2] or Esusu[2] in Nigeria, the traditional saving schemes typically have a few independent individuals contribute cash and take turns to receive a pay-out of the total amount in the purse during the savings cycle. These schemes are as popular in the informal sector as they are in the professional sector. The only difference between a traditional scheme and an investment club is, when cash is contributed in an investment club, it is invested in assets or business projects. The returns on such investments are paid out as dividend or profit to the members of the club.

When we started our investment club, we had no formal framework. Over a 2-year period, we defined guidelines and, eventually, formulated a framework to provide structure as we made investment decisions. During this period, I noticed that anytime I talked about my investment club, I received requests from people seeking to join. At the time, we were not taking on new members, so I decided to create a general framework based on my experience starting and operating an investment club. The aim was so that those requesting to join could pick it up and use it as a guide to start their investment club.

From teaching my framework to over 100 people at three (3) 'How to Invest' workshops[3], having my free e-book downloaded over 700 times on my website[4], and midwifing 15 other investment clubs with my Investment Club Framework™ (ICF), I know that becoming a member of an investment club requires a certain mindset and financial discipline. Not everyone who expresses interest is ready to start or become a member of an investment club.

***

Growing up in Lagos (Nigeria), I was an inquisitive child who got a kick out of trying new things, including my mum's clothes and other things that were off limits. I got away with many of these antics. The others, I wasn't so lucky. One of the antics I found hard to live down in my teenage years was an incident with my mum's brand-new car.

It had been delivered to the house while she was out. My siblings and I eagerly received the car, and my elder sister instructed the driver to park it in the garage. The driver handed over the keys to her while I watched. After he left, I asked my sister for the keys with an innocent comment about wanting to see the interior of the car. She handed it to me, and I rushed to open the door on the driver's side. I took a seat.

"I am going to turn on the car engine," I told her.

"Do you know what you're doing?" My sister, ever the careful one, asked.

"Yes," I said boldly, putting the key into the ignition and turning on the car engine. To my excitement, I heard it roar to a start. That was my first time turning on a car engine. Before then, all I had done was watch my parents drive.

Excited by my smooth success so far, I put the car in gear. To my utmost shock, the car jerked back. I had put it in reverse mode. I scrambled to return the gear to its former position, but the damage had already been done. I had left the car door open when I put the car in reverse mode, and the door got hooked on a shelf in our garage and bent backwards. My whole life played before my eyes. I knew I was in grave trouble and there was no way I could hide the damage or deny the act. Let's just say, I got the worst punishment ever doled out by my parents.

That incident, however, taught me to study anything I wanted to be good at. When I made up my mind to get better at managing my money and started an investment club, I knew I had taken steps in the right direction; however, I soon realized that continuing that journey required constant study. When my investment club lost money on a few deals, I knew it was time to study how investing really works. I realized that making investment decisions was more than contributing money and investing in random opportunities.

I pored over articles online, took out time to read books, sent emails to experts requesting to glean from their wealth of knowledge, attended conferences, and did a lot of research to know all I know today. Yet, I am quick to acknowledge that I am on a journey.

"I don't think I need to know too much or dig deep," you might think. "I can always get an investment advisor."

You're right. You can. But reflect on this. I eventually had to attend driving lessons to learn how to drive. I was taught the basics and, now, I drive confidently. I didn't attend my driving lessons to learn how to race in Formula One. All I needed to learn was how to drive a basic car so as to avoid car accidents and not depend on someone else to drive me all the time. That's the same way you should approach learning about investing. You don't have to become an investment manager if you're not interested in that line of career; all you need to learn are the basics to feel comfortable with making investment decisions or approving those made on your behalf.

Does my story sound familiar? Have you ever wondered about how to make an investment decision or how to collaborate on an investment opportunity? Have you thought about how to start an investment club effectively? The good news is you are reading the right book. The not-too-good news is collaborations are not for the faint hearted. You must be willing to step out of your comfort zone and take some risks.

Getting Started with Personal Flows

This was not my normal routine.

Since I stopped working full time, I spend the best part of my day creating content and products that help subscribers to my email list make better investment decisions. I got the email invite the day before and decided it might not be a bad idea to get out of my comfort zone and attend the event, especially since it was a networking event for millennials.

The first person I met at the event was Simi. When I walked into the room, I couldn't help but notice Simi talking and laughing with a few people at the other end of the room. I found the cocktail bar and immediately grabbed a glass as I scanned the room to see if there was any familiar face. That's when I noticed Simi walking up to me. She introduced herself and we got talking. I told her one of the things I do is work with professionals who wanted to learn how to make better investment decisions and she sighed, 'I think I need your help.'

She was not entirely proud of how she had managed her money the previous year and she wanted this year to be different. "The only thing I did really well, last year, was spend money on Aso-ebi to support my friends', she laughed. As the year came to an end, her reality stared her in the face, she was broke and it was time get her money act together.

"I've had enough," she insisted. "It's time to stop spending money impulsively. Surely, there must be a simple way to put together a budget to track my spending."

I agreed to work with her and we started with the herculean task of tracking how she spent money, what she discovered surprised her. Her job in a multinational organisation ensured that, by any comparative measure, she was well compensated; yet, she couldn't see how she would achieve her investment goal with what she was earning. It seemed like her income got cleaned out of her bank account as soon as she got paid.

The essential first step for anyone interested in becoming a member of an investment club is a personal review of what I call the flows: cash inflow and outflow. It might sound cliché, but it is a fundamental step. Take a couple of hours in a calm environment to outline a summary of your cash inflow and outflow for a defined period (weekly or monthly) basis. Your cash inflow is income you earn or receive from a job or business, while your cash outflow is any expense you make or gift you give out in monetary terms.

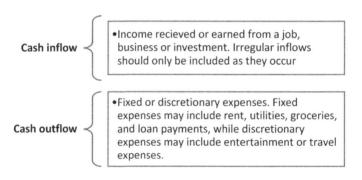

Cash inflow — •Income recieved or earned from a job, business or investment. Irregular inflows should only be included as they occur

Cash outflow — •Fixed or discretionary expenses. Fixed expenses may include rent, utilities, groceries, and loan payments, while discretionary expenses may include entertainment or travel expenses.

Simi's cash inflow consisted only of her monthly salary, which was stable. Her cash outflow, however, was not as stable and, cumulatively, was greater than what she received as inflow. There was a clear problem. There was no way she would have any spare cash to invest if her outflow always exceeded her inflow. If your cash outflow is greater than your inflow, you're clearly at a negative net cash flow every month. It was time to figure out how to solve Simi's problem.

Digging further, we took the next step.

After, reviewing her cash inflows and cash outflows, we took the next step to analyse each outflow or expense line to check for excesses. When Simi did this, she discovered many excesses. Working together, we objectively nipped and tucked at her personal budget until we could create a budget for investing consistently. From assuming it would be impossible to achieve her investment goals, Simi was able to create a budget to live within her income and set aside a defined amount for investing.

This is what I describe as making investing a bill. Investing is and should be a bill; a bit of cash out of each pay-cheque every month invested into an asset class. This habit will require discipline. The discipline of ensuring you live within your means and setting aside an amount to invest on a regular basis. The amount you decide to set aside doesn't really matter; it is the discipline that matters.

Investing regularly is a great way to take advantage of compound interest and build up an essential habit.

Step 1	Step 2	Step 3
Review your cash flows; cash inflows and cash outflows	Analyse each outflow or expense for excesses. Also check to see how to increase inflow	Make investment a bill and start investing or contributing to your investment club

I meet many people who are waiting for a cash windfall before they start investing. That might not be a wise decision. If you keep waiting, you might wait forever. You can start with what you have. Being disciplined and consistent with investing is what tilts the scale in your favor.

Why Should Anyone Invest?

1) **Investing puts your money to work**
   Once, on a radio program, I was asked why anyone needs to put their money to work.

   "You need to put your money to work so that, eventually, it can work for you and you don't have to keep working for the rest of your life," I said.

   We all dream about financial freedom, but if we're ever

going to make our dreams come true, we need to put our money to work. Experts say there are three (3) types of income: Earned Income, Portfolio Income, and Passive Income. Earned income is generated when you put in time and effort to work. Some activities that require time and effort include a "9 to 5" job, owning a small business, consulting, or gambling. Earned income is the most common mechanism for making money, but the obvious downside is that when you stop working, you stop earning.

Earned income, however, can be used to generate portfolio income and passive income. That's what we mean by putting your money to work. Portfolio Income is any income earned from selling an investment for much higher than you paid for it. Paper assets such as equities/stock, bonds, mutual funds, exchange traded funds (ETF), treasury bills, or other forms of securities, are all common forms of earning portfolio income. Buying and selling real estate or any other asset (specifically the profit from sale) also generate portfolio income.

Ever heard about making money while you sleep? That's Passive Income. Passive Income is defined as the recurring income you earn without being actively involved in the activity required to generate income. The central idea is that you put in the work once and continue to earn from that one-off activity long-term. Rental income earned from real estate is a great example for this category of income. If you own a business that could operate independently of your direct supervision, income from that business can be considered passive income as well. Other examples include creating and selling intellectual property, network marketing and dividend income from investment in equities/stock.

If financial independence is a goal for you, then piling up cash in a bank account so you can check your account balance from time to time and pat yourself on the back for keeping millions in your savings account is not what will help you achieve it. Apart from the fact that you are likely to spend money in a savings account when you have access to it, you're also missing out on using cash as a tool. Cash is a tool; you need to use it as a means to an end—your goals. You need to put your cash to work to earn returns.

Earning returns on your investment is better than earning a monthly salary. When you earn your monthly income, you should put it to work in an investment vehicle, so it can earn returns. Ideally, you should work towards living off the profit from returns on your investment vehicle, and not off your monthly income. Investing provides a compounding factor to your cash, and it provides the opportunity to do a lot more than what your pay-cheque can offer you.

2) **Investing helps you mitigate the risk of losing the value of your money.**
If you think about it, not investing is a risk to your cash

in terms of value and buying power. Not giving yourself the opportunity to grow your wealth is almost certainly as risky as being in the financial markets and is riskier over longer time horizons (10-20 years).

A close friend once told me a story about a blue-collared man who decided to save up money so that he could leave an inheritance for his children. He saved for 30 years, carefully depositing the money at the bank monthly and taking time to read his bank statements to ensure it captured the correct amount. At the end of the thirtieth year, he was proud of what he had accomplished, retired, and waited till it was time to hand over the cash inheritance to his children.

When he stopped saving, what he had accumulated could purchase multiple pieces of real estate. However, by the time he died, the inheritance had lost value significantly, due to double-digit inflation, and it was hardly enough to spend on his funeral.

A great way to get your money to work for you is by understanding the relationship between risk and reward. People who say they don't like to take risks are taking a bigger risk by not investing their money. They stand the risk of losing the value of their money until it is not worth, in value terms, the original amount with which they started.

3) **By Investing appropriately, you can create a hedge against Inflation.**

According to Rick Ferri, founder of Advisory Portfolio Solutions, "The first thing you need to do is beat the inflation rate with whatever investment you make. If you don't beat the inflation rate, you're losing, not making money."

In developed countries, inflation rates are typically single digit. The Inflation rate in the United States of America averaged 3.28 percent from 1914 until 2017, reaching an all-time high of 23.70 percent in June of 1920 and a record low of -15.80 percent in June of 1921.[5] In developing countries, they range from mid-single digit to double digit, averaging 4% to 10% typically. National inflation rates vary widely in individual cases.[6] Inflation Rate in Nigeria averaged 12.50 percent from 1996 until 2018, reaching an all-time high of 47.56 percent in January of 1996.[7]

This is why investing your money in a manner that beats inflation is always a good call. The return on an investment is typically determined by the risk associated with the investment opportunity. When it is low risk, you earn low returns, medium risk earns you medium returns, and high risk earns you high returns.

What if I have a limited budget?

I am often asked questions like, "What if I have a limited budget to invest and my goal is to increase my net worth by 100% in a couple of years?"

My standard response is, "Find a group of like-minded people and invest together".

Research shows that most of the wealthy investors we have today didn't achieve their wealth feats by investing alone. They partnered with like-minded people or those who were ready to part with cash to get more cash in return in the future.

Warren Buffet became a millionaire in 1962 because of his investment partnerships.8 He successfully brought together multiple groups of people who were willing to contribute to a joint fund and earn double digit annual interest in return. Over time, the value of the partnerships grew significantly and made him extremely wealthy.
In the next chapter, you'll learn how to go beyond average, and why you should consider investing with others on your investment journey.

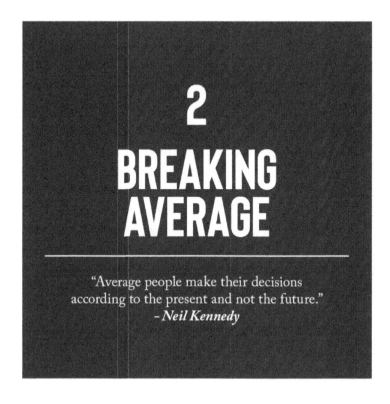

2
BREAKING
AVERAGE

*"Average people make their decisions
according to the present and not the future."*
- Neil Kennedy

On a cool summer evening, five friends and former MBA classmates met in the lobby of a prestigious hotel in Lagos. They had a mission and, together, they crafted a plan to collaborate and invest in fast growing small and medium businesses.

I was one of the five, and my goal was to collaborate my way to financial freedom. I was intent on increasing the investment opportunities I could take advantage of, so that I could increase my chances of achieving financial freedom. I also believed it was a great opportunity to dedicate my professional skills and experience to help growing businesses gain access to capital and implement the right growth strategy.

My friends and I set out with the audacious goal to build wealth by providing medium- to long-term capital to small businesses. We started our investment club to enable the African dream—access to capital for entrepreneurs who can change the bleak African story. Looking back now, I realize we were green-eyed and, like many fresh MBA graduates, we were naïve enough to believe we could change the world. They say it is only those who believe they can change the world that do so. We were willing to take our chances.

Our investment club, Midas Capital, was established in 2013 and has invested in 4 companies and 2 short-term projects spanning four (4) industries in Nigeria. All the founding members are still active members of the club. We started our investment club because we were determined to go beyond our average means.

What Does It Mean to be an Average Investor?

One of my favorite books of all time is George Samuel Clason's 'The Richest Man in Babylon'. It is a collection of parables, or stories if you will, about a group of characters dispensing financial wisdom to aspirational young men who want to be rich. My favorite quote is, "If you want to achieve anything in life, you must make it a study."

Basically, this means that if you want to build a successful business, you must make it a point to study successful businesses and how they continue to be sustainable. If you want to have a successful marriage, you should study successful marriages or books about marriage. In the same vein, if you want to be a successful investor, you should study the intricacies of investing and how the complex world of investing works.

My first attempt to gain an understanding of the intricacies of investing started with reading the book, 'Rich Dad, Poor Dad'. Digging further into his books series, I read the 'Rich Dad's Guide to Investing'. In this book, Robert Kiyosaki asks his rich dad what advice he would give an average investor, and he answers, "Don't be average". Those words struck a chord with me the minute I read them. They described what I have set as a core value for myself for many years. Since that time, I have been on a quest to understand what it means to be average and worked to not be an average investor.

So far, I have come up with three (3) definitions of an average investor,

1) **An average investor invests without a plan.**
   Investing is not a product; it is a plan. An average investor invests in random investment opportunities that promise good returns. However, an educated investor has a plan, understands his/her risk tolerance level, and knows the investment options required to arrive at the defined destination.

Sometimes, when I travel, I take connecting flights to my destination. On a recent trip to the USA from Nigeria, I took a flight to Casablanca with a plan to board a connecting flight from Casablanca to New York. My flight ticket stated New York, USA, as my destination and I finally arrived at my destination after 21+ hours in transit. Now, compare my itinerary with that of someone who boarded a direct flight from Nigeria to the USA. That person will arrive at his/her destination in less time—about 5 hours—than I spent in transit.

For reasons ranging from a cheaper ticket to the chance to experience another vacation spot or travelling with little children, I took a route that increased the hours it would take to arrive in the USA. However, what was important was: I knew my destination and I had figured out a way to arrive there on my own terms. Someone else who took a direct flight also had a planned destination and took a route that suited their lifestyle, budget, and time preferences.

When you make investment decisions, you should be aware that investing is YOUR route plan to YOUR destination, based on your life stage, risk tolerance, budget, and other variables. You shouldn't focus on the vehicle of transport and lose sight of your destination. Keep your destination in sight and choose the 'vehicles' that will help you arrive in one piece.

Don't get attached to the 'vehicles', create a plan that works for you.

2) An average investor invests as an individual and not as a business owner

Investing as an individual—in your own name—is great but not smart investing. The best way to invest is to have your business make investments or buy assets for you. This is what rich people do to protect their assets and save on tax. They build businesses that own assets and pay most of their business and personal expenses.

Think of it this way, when you invest as an individual, you invest with post-tax income; however, when you invest as a business, you can invest with pre-tax income. Your investment cost can sit as an expense line on your financial statements. This is why investment clubs are great. You get to collaborate with like-minded people with similar goals and invest as a business. There are different options to invest as a business and we'll delve into it in chapter 3. However, it is best to review your investment expenses with a tax advisor so that you can maximize the deductions available to you through your business.

3) An average investor thinks in terms of income and not net worth

Income earned can easily trickle away if not preserved. When you measure your wealth only in terms of the cash that sits in your bank account, you are susceptible to inflationary pressures and the volatility in the value of the currency in which your cash is kept. However, if you think in terms of net-worth, your wealth is captured in investment vehicles (assets) that can appreciate and probably stand the test of time, in terms of value. Your net-worth is therefore composed mainly of the assets in which you have preserved and accumulated your income over time.

Again, an investment club offers you an opportunity to build up your net-worth over time with like-minded people.

What is an Investment Club?

An investment club is a group of people who consolidate funds to invest in deals and business opportunities as one entity. It offers members a great opportunity to share risks and rewards in a way that contributes to the growth of common wealth in the society.

An investment club offers everyone a win/win solution. If you consider your funds limited in anyway, you can start an investment club with friends and, together, you can take advantage of investing with the pooled funds.

Where Did Investment Clubs Begin?

In 1951, Tom O'Hara and his investing friends got the vision to start an investing movement of investment clubs, which they named the National Association of Investment Clubs (NAIC). Tom O'Hara had started his investment club (Mutual club of Detroit) in February 1948 with $20 monthly dues. This club has since grown into an organization of over 37,000 investment clubs with 478,000 active participants.[1]

According to Better Investing (also known as the National Association of Investors Corporation USA), investment clubs date back to the late 19th century. The oldest known investment club, still in operation today, is the Hamilton Trust, an investment club created in Boston in January 1882.[2]

The next-oldest known club began operations in Texas in 1898. Most of the early clubs were formed as social organizations, with combined investing as one activity. Based on information captured in 1958 by the National Association of Investment Clubs (NAIC), there was little, if any, attempt to establish uniform principles for the guidance and education of members of investment clubs until recently.[3]

In Nigeria, one of the most successful pioneering investment clubs is Investments (1971) Limited. This investment club was established by a group of educated elites in Lagos. They all socialised extensively at social functions and social clubs such as Klub Executives, a prominent social club back in the day. Many prominent members of Klub Executives became the founding members of Investments (1971) Limited. The investment club started with 50 members, 10 of whom withdrew membership at various times for various reasons. However, Investments (1971) still thrives today and celebrated 45 years of existence in 2017.[4]

***

In Africa, traditional savings contributory schemes are more common than investment clubs. These contributory schemes encourage a savings culture within communities by enabling a cycle of pooling and disbursing bulk funds to those who contribute to these schemes. The traditional name for this scheme is Ajo/Esusu. The Yoruba word, 'Ajo', translated literally, means 'pooling resources together'.

Women in traditional markets have long taken advantage of the power of many with the Ajo scheme. Most of these women lacked basic education and, thus, did not operate bank accounts. The Ajo was a way to contribute to a purse and get access to 'credit' for stock purchase or basic living expenses. These traditional schemes still exist and can now be found in both formal and informal work environments today.

I have participated in some of these schemes before, and my experience was always a good one. Without hassles, I received my funds whenever my turn in the cycle came up. However, when the economy took a turn, during one of such cycles, I got wiser. The Naira (local Nigerian currency) lost value to the dollar and it became clear that I was losing the value of my money by just saving and getting paid once my turn in the cycle came up. I was losing the value of my money to inflation and volatility in the value of the currency as well.

It was clear that it was better to invest my money and not simply leave it in a holding system that gave me cash when I needed it.

Investment clubs to the rescue

As stated earlier in the book, before business school, I worked for 4+ years in a boutique consulting firm, where I earned a pretty good salary. However, I was not deliberate with financial planning and did more spending than I probably should have. After all, to my naïve self, I was young, and retirement was still far away.

When it was time to begin my MBA at the Lagos Business School (LBS), it struck me that I wouldn't earn an income over the next 24 months and, even worse, I hadn't built up any savings to lean on.

Thankfully, I survived my MBA with support from the right quarters, and I graduated with a resolve to get myself on a sustainable path towards financial independence. I wanted to create wealth for myself and impact my community simultaneously. Initially, the biggest hurdle was saving enough capital to start investing immediately. That's when I realized it would be great to pool funds with other people and invest as an entity.

The benefits were:

1) **Investing larger amounts**

   We started with each member contributing N50,000 ($300 at N165/$[5]) monthly and worked together to identify investment opportunities. The focus, at the beginning, was to develop the discipline of consistently contributing to the fund so that, as it grew, we could invest in larger investment opportunities than we would have been able to individually.

   Our first investment was in a transport company that provided pick-up and drop-off services to young professionals. Our investment allowed the company to expand its fleet and we realized strong monthly cash flows into the fund. I would not have been able to do this on my own within a year of completing my MBA and with access to only 20% of the fund's original investment.

2) **Sharing the risks**

   Our investment club allowed us to limit the downside risk of each investment. Note that I did not say eliminate risk — we have had our share of losses, both in the stock market and in private investment deals. However, pooling funds minimized individual losses.

In addition, the collaborative investment approach mitigates the risk of information asymmetry (limited knowledge) that exists when one is investing individually.

3) **Gaining practical investment experience**
As a group, we benefitted immensely from the diversity of our skills and experience. None of us had prior professional investing experience, but the journey of discovering new insights has been rewarding. We learned not to invest based on sentiments or random decisions. We had to agree on a well-thought-out process for considering how an investment opportunity adds value and can provide healthy returns to our fund.

One of the great benefits of investing as a club is that each member brings a different approach to analysing investment decisions, which others benefit from. That would not be possible if one invested alone. We also leveraged on the weight of our club to gain access to experts in industries, gather specialized knowledge, and gain goodwill that ultimately led us to making better investment decisions.

4) **Being accountable on the journey**
Sometimes, it was tough to contribute to a fund from which I did not receive dividends. There were days when I wanted to call it quits but being accountable to my investment club kept me going. Each month, I

choose to stay committed because of my goals, and being on the journey with like-minded people helps.

To stay committed to your investing goals, you will need an accountability system. That's because it is tough to keep setting aside money to invest for the future. On this journey, you will need a lot of discipline and commitment to keep contributing your hard-earned cash as a member of an investment club. Being accountable to the other members of your club will help in this regard.

How the Onans' Broke Average

The Onans' were a young couple living in the United Kingdom (UK). They were interested in putting the cash they earned to better use, but they had no experience investing. Not willing to give up because they didn't have any experience investing, they decided to read up on all the asset classes to see which one they would be comfortable with or, at least, could start with. In their own words, "We chose to invest in the property market (real estate) but soon realized we didn't have enough money to get started. However, we knew we had to find a way to generate passive income if we were ever going to be financially free".

They were presented with the option to spend years saving up to invest on their own by the banks and financial advisers but after speaking with a few people who were in the same situation as they were, they decided to set up a joint venture. That was the beginning of their investment club.

"Three (3) couples (6 members in total) decided to pool our money, ideas and expertise with the help of appropriate UK property experts. Each member had strengths and interests which informed role delegations within the club. Each member handled a role they enjoyed and could perform effectively. The roles included; researching location and type of properties, sorting out the best financial or mortgage companies, dealing with the property experts, planning and administration of the club". In the first year of existence, they purchased 4 properties off-plan and below market value; 1 property in Essex, 2 properties in Manchester and 1 property in Leeds.

The investment club helped the Onans' and other members get on the property ladder in the UK quicker than they would have if they had tried to invest individually.

Is an Investment Club Right for Me?

There are certain questions I get often:

- Is an investment club the right step for me?
- Can it help me achieve financial freedom?

My response is always another question: *Do you work well in teams?*

If you have always wished there was a way you could do more or achieve more with the funds you have, then you should consider investment clubs. If you fit into all or any of the profiles described below, then you may just be the right candidate for an investment club.

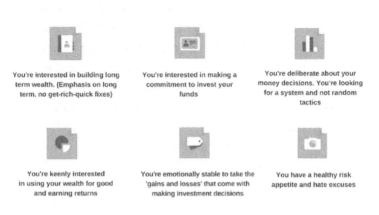

You're interested in building long term wealth. (Emphasis on long term, no get-rich-quick fixes)

You're interested in making a commitment to invest your funds

You're deliberate about your money decisions. You're looking for a system and not random tactics

You're keenly interested in using your wealth for good and earning returns

You're emotionally stable to take the 'gains and losses' that come with making investment decisions

You have a healthy risk appetite and hate excuses

An investment club takes a collaborative approach to making investment decisions. Members pool resources together and share both the risks and rewards of investing. It provides a great learning opportunity—being part of a team makes it easier to learn from the diversity of skills and professional experiences of other members.

What are My Options?

Nobody likes to be stuck without options, so you will be pleased to learn there are different models of investment clubs. Investment clubs in my network, Club 360 operate one or two of these models. Club 360 is a network of investment clubs. It provides an easy way to learn from the mistakes and success stories of the other clubs in the network. No investment club should exist in isolation; you should tap into the power of a network. You can adapt any of the models to that which is preferred by the members of your club.

1) **The Financial Model**

   This is the base model of investment clubs. In a financial investment club, each member contributes to a common purse. Traditional investment clubs implement the base model.

   Investments (1971) Limited implemented this base model successfully for 45 years. They started with contributing 25 pounds monthly in July 1971 and evolved into paying each member annual dividends in 2003.

   When we started our investment club, we decided to contribute funds to a common purse from inception, just like Investments (1971) Limited. We had just concluded our MBA program, and we were eager to start. We all made investment a bill and built up our club's funds over time. We have consistently contributed to the common purse this way for 4+ years, and we fund investment opportunities from the common purse.

There are two types of financial investment clubs: the term-based investment club and the project-based investment club.

The term-based investment club has a defined period of existence. It may be defined as a fixed number of years or defined in multiple investment phases. My investment club defined a 5-year term for the first phase of our investment club, after which we will review and agree on our next steps. One of the clubs in my network, based in Ghana, defined a 10-year term for the first phase of their club, after which they plan to go on a joint vacation. I guess all investment and no play makes a dull club. This doesn't mean you have to define a fixed period of existence if you prefer not to; you can establish fixed periods to review your investment portfolio and plan for the next phase instead.

The project-based investment club is created based on a specific project or asset of interest. Members of a project-based investment club contribute funds to invest in a certain project/asset class. Once the project is completed, the investment club may cease to exist.

In August 2017, I launched a project-based investment

club with 52 members. It was created specifically to invest in real estate. It is not an easy feat to manage 52 members in an investment club. It is, however, easier to manage than a financial investment club because it is project-based. A project-based investment club is temporary; it is focused on completing an investment cycle, after which it may cease to exist. Over the course of managing the affairs of this club, I have learnt a lot about the real estate industry in Nigeria just like I learnt a lot about investing when we started our investment club 5 years ago. Nothing beats experiential education; an investment club offers this in truckloads if you're open-minded.

Characteristics of the 'Financial model'

A. **Members contribute financially to a common purse**

The main advantage of operating a financial model for your investment club is that you get to pool funds with other members and invest in opportunities as a group for a defined period or for life. This provides leverage to take advantage of bigger investment opportunities and earn higher returns as well.

B. **Members make investment decisions together.**

My investment club, Midas capital, had to develop an investment guideline to guide our investment decisions. The investment guide or framework outlines the club's investment philosophy, investment strategy, and the types of transactions we were interested in as a club (more details in chapter 3). If you decide to start a financial investment club, your investment decisions should be guided by defined investment guidelines. That's because all members may not always agree on an investment decision.

2) The Non-Financial Model

The non-financial investment club is strictly an accountability group. Members of the club jointly review and analyse investment opportunities, but actual investing is done individually.

When I blogged about my investment club on my website, I received many emails with questions about investment clubs and how they worked. This led me to create the investment club framework. Sharing the framework led to another discovery: not everyone is keen on investing with others.

After deep consideration, I created the Green Club and launched it as a platform for those who want to get started investing and learn with other beginner investors in a community. In the Green Club, I teach the members how to make good investment decisions via an online course and share investment opportunities for them to get started immediately. We also have strategic partnerships with the following companies: a licensed stockbroking firm, a real estate company, and a wealth management company, to facilitate investment transactions swiftly for members of the Green Club. The focus of the Green Club is to get as many beginner investors as possible started on their investment journey with minimal issues.

I launched the pilot program for the Green Club successfully in August 2017, with 35 members. The Green Club exists strictly as an accountability group and currently has 100+ members from 5 countries: Nigeria, South Africa, Cameroun, Dubai, and the UK.

Visit *www.tomiebalogun.com/the-green-club/* to find out more about the green club.

Characteristics of the 'Non-financial model'

A. Members do not contribute financially to the club
Members of this group simply meet regularly to discuss investment goals and learn from one another's experience. The social interaction provided by the regular meetings motivates members to set aside funds to invest. If the members decide to take the step to make financial contributions and invest together as a club, they become a financial investment club.[5]

B. Members do not make investment decisions together

The group exists to hold its members accountable to investment goals they set together. However, they are not required to make investment decisions together. Each member is free to decide in favour of or against an investment opportunity. (See appendix for sample guidelines for non-financial investment clubs)

3) The Business Model

This is an interesting model. It is implemented when members of an investment club choose to start a business venture i.e. act as co-founders and co-investors in an actual start-up. This can be a tough model to execute, as members need to be fully engaged or employ full time staff to keep the business in operation. In addition, implementing a member's exit might be a problem. One of the clubs in my network tried to execute this but it did not work out successfully, so they had to revert to the base model. It was unsuccessful because they were all fully engaged in full time employment and could not dedicate the time required to get a start-up into operation mode.

4) The Hybrid Model

The hybrid model is a combination of any of the three models: financial, non-financial, and/or business. One of the investment clubs in our network included an additional feature of a savings contributory scheme at inception to get its members used to setting money aside on a regular basis. Payments were made to the members in cycles like the traditional Ajo/Esusu, while they prepared for eventual transition into being a financial investment club with investment education. This model gave the club members the opportunity to engage as a team and then decide if they wanted to go the long haul and be part of a proper investment club before investment activities commenced.

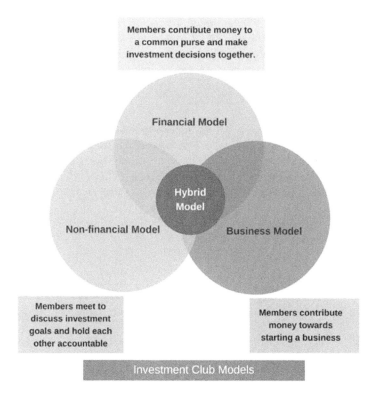

When making a decision on a model for your investment club, ensure you know exactly what you're getting into and with whom you will be investing. If you have friends you believe can stay together and weather the storm of gains and losses, it is ok to start a financial investment club with them.

If you are not completely sure about this, you can start an accountability group (the non-financial model) to test the waters. In an accountability group, you can all set investment goals, discuss them, learn about investment options, and hold one another accountable. (See sample guidelines for a non-financial accountability group in appendix.)

You may also want to consider the hybrid model where the club starts with a savings contributory scheme (Ajo or Esusu). Starting with this scheme will allow members to get used to the habit of setting money aside regularly. Once they are used to saving on a regular basis, you can then evolve into a financial investment club.

The Investment Club Framework ™

Over the next three (3) chapters, I will walk you through my proprietary framework, the Investment Club Framework (ICF). This framework served as a guide for investment clubs in I have worked it over the past few years. I developed this framework from my personal experience managing my investment club, learning from industry experts and interacting with other clubs in Nigeria, UK, USA, Ghana and Kenya.

The ICF provides a guide on how to start your investment club on the right note, manage effectively the resources of each member of the club to build wealth, invest in a way that diversifies your risks and earns rewards and finally, grow effectively and make an impact on society.

Value Creation

START
- Membership
- Legal structure
- Contribution

ALIGNED GOALS

GROW
- Team dynamics
- Asset Principle
- Networking & Learning

MANAGE
- Roles
- Book keeping
- House keeping

INVEST
- Investment philosophy
- Investment strategy
- Investment process

Value Capture

PART 1

HOW TO START
YOUR INVESTMENT
CLUB

The Investment Club Framework ™

Leveraging resources to build wealth together, spread risks,
gain rewards and make an impact on society.

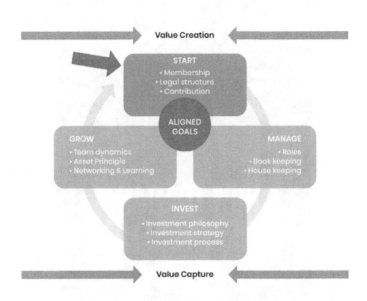

3
THE ART OF
THE START

"Start doing what is necessary; then do what's
possible, then suddenly you'll find
yourself doing the impossible."
- *Francis of Assisi*

When you start a business venture, you know there are
going to be some risks but if you've ever started a new
business venture, you'll know that the challenges you
prepare for or get educated about are rarely the ones that
stop you in your tracks. It's the challenges you don't
predict happening that can really crush you. It's the same
way with investment clubs and this is why nothing beats
learning from experience.

The Guilt of Friendship

Dani is spontaneous and full of life—you could easily chat with her all night at a boring dinner party. Growing up, she loved dancing and reading; she wrote her first book at the age of 10. Dani was her father's favorite, and in his eyes, she could do no wrong. Her family made it a tradition to travel for summer holidays every year, until tragedy struck. In retrospect, Dani couldn't really remember when the tide turned.

"We had to change schools abruptly and start taking public transportation to school," Dani recollects. "My daddy also became ill during that period and it seemed things just went from bad to worse with our finances and we couldn't afford our previous lifestyle anymore."

This experience scarred Dani in so many ways that she became determined to succeed financially, but not for the reasons you might think.

Her best friend, Lilian, had experienced quite the opposite. She attended a school in a middle-class and safe neighbourhood. She did not have to take a bus to school; it was just a couple of blocks away from her modest house. She loved walking to school every day and taking in the everyday realities of growing families in her neighbourhood. They had the basic amenities in her house.

"My parents always taught us to be content and aspire to make an impact on society," says Lilian.

Dani and Lilian met on the first day of work and their friendship blossomed. After a couple of months, Lilian noticed Dani was always broke and requesting loans. She thought it strange, as it did not seem like Dani had any responsibility apart from taking care of herself. They earned the same salary and she always had an amount of money to set aside to save while Dani always requested for a loan by mid-month.

A year into working together, Lilian got educated about the benefits of starting an investment club, and she asked Dani if she was interested in starting one with her. Dani was not keen, but she gave in to please her friend. Lilian seemed so excited about starting an investment club and although Dani didn't get what the excitement was about, she felt obligated to help.

Together, they convinced three more friends to join the club and they were off to a start. They got expert guidance and pretty much thought they had all the requirements for a successful club covered. They named their investment club 'The Fivers'.

Four months into starting the investment club, Dani couldn't meet up with her club contributions anymore. She missed the deadline for payment. Lilian thought it was a temporary situation and decided not to confront her. When Dani missed the deadline for the next month's payment again, Lilian decided it was time to find out what the problem was. Not wanting to make it a big deal, she took Dani out to lunch in hopes of finding out what the problem was.

After a long conversation about work and each other's love life, Lilian asked Dani why she had missed the deadline for club contributions for two months.

Dani went quiet for a few seconds, and then said, "I had a couple of unexpected expenses and couldn't meet up with my contributions. I'll pay up the backlog next month."

Relieved to hear her say this, Lilian encouraged her and changed the subject to a light-hearted one.

At the end of that month, Dani missed the payment deadline again. Lilian had no idea what action to take. She and Dani had been friends longer than any of the other members. She didn't feel it was right to simply ask her to stop being a member of the club, but how long could they possibly allow Dani to keep defaulting on her club contributions?

We have all experienced the guilt of friendship. We assume it is easy to start an investment club with friends or people with whom we share interests. My personal experience in my investment club and helping others get started suggests this is not the case. By the end of this chapter, you will learn how to start your investment club the right way and avoid the common pitfalls.

How Do I Find the Right Members for my Club?

One of the underrated benefits of an MBA program is that you meet and network with like-minded individuals. It was easy for me to identify those with whom I could start an investment club because we had worked together on different class projects and had the chance to see one another at work over a two-year period. We were friends and, largely, knew one another's strengths and weaknesses.

Friends can make great members for your investment club, but the success of your club will depend on how well you work together and how objective you all will be about making investment decisions. You need people who are ready and willing to contribute to the success of the club, not shed work or skip responsibility.

When I asked the members of some of the clubs in my network how they identified the right members for their clubs, a member of the D818 club wrote:

> *I started an investment club with my trusted friends because I felt safer and more confident to go on an investment journey leveraging on our collective strengths and being accountable to like-minded people. I did not want to go on the investment journey alone. I wanted teammates and I do not regret the friends that I agreed to go on this journey with. Pooling our funds together has been*

a great blessing. I have come to respect the discipline and loyalty we all bring to the club. I am glad an investment club gave me the opportunity to experience my friends on a different level.

What she wrote suggests they got their investment club off to a great start and things stayed perfect. It didn't. A couple of months into the investment club, the D818 club experienced some member exits. Obviously, starting an investment club with friends is not the only requirement for a successful investment club.

When identifying the right members for your investment club, here are some questions and comments to aid objectivity:

I.   Is this person objective or does he/she get extremely emotional, especially when money is involved?

II. Does this person have integrity? Do a quick check-in by asking friends about this person's money habits. If this person borrows a lot, for instance, that might be a red flag.

III. Is this person forward-looking and disciplined? Do they consciously try to learn new things? Are they open-minded? Are they disciplined with keeping information?

IV. How do they make decisions? On-the-go or after thorough research of facts? This will help you understand the role this person can play in the club.

V. Is this person a team player? Do they isolate themselves and form cliques? If a person isolates himself or herself often, that red flag might threaten the unity of the club.
VI. What are this person's values? Check to know you can relate to their values, so as to avoid needless clashes.

These questions may seem subjective and provide subjective answers as well. This is why I always suggest members keep an open mind and get a review or analysis of character by talking to a few friends not in your immediate circle, who know this person quite well and can be objective.

How Nadia made her investment club work

In discussions with a senior colleague, Nadia found out about an exciting real estate investment opportunity. The real estate opportunity was a new development in an emerging axis of Lagos, Nigeria; a land reclamation plan to create new land by the state government. History shows that when land is reclaimed by raising the elevation of a waterbed, it becomes a prime location that appreciates in value fast. Nadia knew she didn't want to miss out on this opportunity. However, the cost per plot, $99,000, was way above what she could afford even if she made all the financial sacrifices.

Not willing to give up, she reached out to a few friends and shared the opportunity with them. Prior to learning about this opportunity, she had dabbled into some real estate deals that did not work out. One of the key lessons she learned from those bad deals was that she had to put together a strong team of people who were keenly interested in investing and had the staying power to stick to the transaction till it was concluded.

In her words, "I was very particular about those I shared the opportunity with. I looked out for key qualities such as integrity, knowledge, and expertise. I reached out to a lawyer and real estate expert knowing we would need that expertise. I also reached out to those I knew had the financial discipline and commitment to stick to a long-term transaction." This worked out well as she and 15 friends successfully started an investment club with all the relevant agreements and purchased four (4) premium plots of land in that suburb axis of Lagos. Over the course of the project-based investment, only two members had to exit involuntarily, and they were always easily replaced because of the good structure they had created in the club.

Two years later, the plots of land they purchased at $198,000 are valued at $500,000. Finding the right people who believed in the vision and were willing to make commitment to an investment opportunity increased Nadia's net worth significantly.

Is There an Ideal Number of Members for an Investment Club?

An investment club can have as many members it believes it has the capacity to manage. In specific cases, the investment project may require a specific number of members to get started. The law limits members (shareholders) of a Private Limited Liability Company to a maximum of fifty (50) members/shareholders, while the members of a General Partnership are limited to Twenty (20).

However, I advise you keep club membership to a maximum of twelve (12) persons and a minimum of five (5), for two reasons: It's easier to manage 5-12 people and get them to agree to a shared investment objective, and if you're too few, you may need to contribute a lot more money to make any significant investments.

When my friends and I decided to start an investment club, seven (7) people initially indicated interest in becoming members; however, only five (5) members eventually went through with starting the club, and we have stayed the course. It was a similar story with one of the investment clubs in Club 360:

> *We started our club with 7 members but currently have only 4 members. Some members decided to exit the club and it made the rest of us ask ourselves the tough question, "Why are we in this?" We all*

had to be objective about why we wanted to continue being members of the investment clubs. We realized this was business and not just friendship, when we had to let go of 3 friends. Afterwards, we discussed issues openly and objectively, knowing our initial 'romance' was officially over.

You may accept new members into your club after inception. In considering how to nominate a new member, consciously make a decision based on the value that person brings to the table, in terms of access to investment opportunities and networking. The capacity to make financial contributions should not be your only criteria.

Why Do We need to Agree on an Investment Objective for the Club?

Once you find like-minded people for your club, you need to take this next step. It provides the foundation for all your investment decisions. Your investment objective will determine all your actions and efforts towards investment-related activities.

When I and my friends started our investment club, we all agreed to set up the club to invest in viable business opportunities, but we didn't define a core objective that would guide future investment decisions. This gap became clear when we had to decide on some investment opportunities. Some of us believed it was ok to invest in an aggressive opportunity because we needed to grow our funds significantly, while the rest of us thought it was too risky and thought it wise to preserve capital.

Answering the following important questions will help you define an investment objective:

1) Is the objective of our investment club to build long-term wealth or earn short-term dividends?
The answer to this will determine what investment options you take advantage of as a club. Long-term wealth requires investment in long-term sustainable assets. These assets might not be easy to liquidate on short notice; however, you are assured of a sizeable appreciation in value over time.

Short-term dividends will require a different mindset. When club members want to pay out returns earned rather than plough it back to grow the fund, they are interested in short-term dividends. They will have to consider keeping their assets in short-term investment options or short-term business deals to make this happen on a regular basis.

You may also decide to allocate your funds to long term assets and short-term assets in ratios that work with your overall investment goal. Take for example, investing 60% of your funds in long term investment options and 40% in short term options. It all depends on your objective as a club.

2) **What is the defined period for our investment club?**
An investment club can exist until infinity or for a defined period. An ideal timeline to measure the growth of your club is 5 years. This period gives you time to understand one other as members of a club, learn how to make investment decisions together, and grow your funds significantly.

You may choose to define a longer period. Please ensure you discuss and provide comprehensive answers to the following questions:

I.   How long will all members keep contributing to the club's funds?
II. Do you plan to continue investing for the entire period the investment club exists or for a shorter time?
III. If your club invests in long-term assets, how do you plan to liquidate the funds after the defined period? Sell them off or keep them as assets for longer?

3) **Do we pay one another dividends regularly or plough back profit into club funds?**
In a financial investment club, members make financial contributions and expect to earn returns on investment. This may get a little tricky if all club members do not decide, from inception, if they want to

get paid in dividends on a regular basis or prefer to plough back profit earned into the club funds. You want to avoid a situation where, after earning profit, some members begin to make requests for pay-outs.

Dividend payments may not give the club an opportunity to maximize the growth of its funds. However, if the members decide to pay out dividends, that is ok. An option to consider might be holding off on paying out dividends until the defined period for the investment club ends.

It is important to discuss and agree on an investment goal or objective for your club, as this may make or mar future investment decisions. Differing views should be discussed openly and analysed before club operations commence.

In the words of one of the co-founders of my investment club:

Start your club with friends with similar investment goals. This will make investment decisions easier to make. You must also be patient. It can be a long and tedious journey. There will, most likely, not be instant gratification or glory. However, having a very clear objective and mindset from the start will assist greatly in the high and low seasons of your journey.

How Do We Take on New Members in Our Investment Club?

Ideally, existing members of the club should base the election of a new member on a 'no objection' agreement. When a new member indicates interest in joining your investment club, ask them to be nominated by an active existing member of the club.

Two other existing members can second the nomination. Subject to acceptance by all members, the new member may be accepted. However, note the following:

I.   The club reserves the right to refuse admission to any person without giving a reason.
II.   On acceptance to the club, new members may be asked to either:
    a. Pay contributions equal in value to total contributions made by a founding member of the club i.e. the total sum of money contributed by an individual club member from inception of the club;
    b. Or start making contributions from the month of joining the club and get shares allocated by the club (per the agreed capital structure) accordingly.

How Do We Manage Member Exits?

When Dani missed the payment deadline for four months, Lilian knew it was time to act. It is always sad to see a member leave the investment club, but life happens. Continuous payment default can hurt the morale of your investment club much more than a member exit can. This is why you might need to have some tough conversations. Every club should establish guidelines to manage a member exit if or when it occurs. Managing this process effectively will ensure the other members stick together, if they so decide, and continue to exist as a club.

When a member of the club decides to exit the club either voluntarily or involuntarily, the following guidelines may be applied:

I.   Any member may withdraw a part or all the value of his contribution in the club and the club shall continue as a legal entity. Note that for companies or partnership structures, at least 2 people must participate in the entity.

II.   A member who intends to exit should provide a notice of intent to withdraw to the other members of the club and call for a meeting where the exit will be discussed and signed off by the remaining members.

III. If the withdrawing member intends to withdraw a part or all the value of his contributions, the member should give notice of the intention to withdraw in writing to the club. Written notice to withdraw can be shared via email.

In making payment to the withdrawing member, a current version of the value of the club should be used to determine the value of the member's account. The club should pay the member who is withdrawing a portion or total value of his/her contribution in accordance with the following guidelines:

I.   In the case of a partial withdrawal, payment can be made in cash, kind, or securities of the club or a mix of each at the option of the member making the partial withdrawal.

II.   In the case of a full withdrawal, payment should be made in cash, kind, or securities or a mix at the option of the remaining members. In either case, where securities are to be distributed, the remaining members should select the securities.

III.   The club should transfer to the member (or other appropriate entity) withdrawing a portion or total value of his interest in the club, an amount equal to the value of the contributions being withdrawn, less any actual expenses to the club related to the withdrawal.

IV.   If the member withdrawing a portion or total value of his contribution in the club desires an immediate payment in cash, the club, at its earliest convenience, may decide to pay a percentage of the estimated value of his contribution and settle the balance in accordance with the valuation and agreed payment procedures by the club.

V. An outgoing member is not entitled to any share or interest in the property or profits of the club earned after exit.

For one of the investment clubs in my network, it was a bittersweet story when a member of their close-knit club decided to exit. While they felt emotional about her decision, they knew it was time to make some tough calls—chief of which was how to manage a fair pay-out. Prior to this, they didn't have an exit clause in the investment agreement, so they had to come up with one to manage the situation.

The club's investment portfolio was allocated to multiple investment options, most of which could not be easily liquidated to get the cash required to pay-out the withdrawing member. After deliberations, they decided to pay the withdrawing member from future contributions of the other members of the investment club.

For a project-focused investment club in the UK, it was a different story. The principal asset class they invested in was real estate. Together, they had contributed funds to invest in prime real estate and looked forward to earning significant rewards together. When two members decided to withdraw as members of the club, it came as a shock. It was an involuntary exit as these two members were relocating to a different country. The other members had to come up with the cash contribution for the withdrawing members and pay back over a period.

In both cases, managing the sudden exit of members forced the clubs to make tough decisions. However, the exit process could have been managed better if they had agreed on exit guidelines from inception.

From experience, most investment clubs are not able to immediately pay off the member who decides to exit. When this is the case, members of the investment club provide a tentative date to the withdrawing member to make the contribution pay-out or agree on a pay-out plan with the member who decides to exit.

Do We Need to Register Our Investment Club as a Legal Entity?

Yes, you do. It might seem like a bother, but because money is a sensitive issue, it is best handled within the confines of a legal entity. A legal structure makes your investment club a legally recognized entity, and it ensures that all members are formally identified as shareholders or partners.

All members of the club need to agree on the legal entity of choice. The function of your club should determine the form adopted. There are four (4) factors to consider before you decide on the legal structure to adopt. They include:

1. Liability (Do you want to have limited or unlimited liability)
2. Governance (How do you want the club to be managed?)
3. Tax obligations (How will you fulfil your tax obligations?)
4. Membership (How many members would the club have?).

The following provides an overview of the legal options available to an investment club.

Investment Club Registration Options

1) General Partnership (GP)

A General Partnership is the basic form of partnership; it provides equal business and personal liability for every partner. The owners of a partnership invest their own funds and time in the business, and they share, proportionally, any profits earned by the entity as per Partnership Agreement.

The roles and responsibilities of each partner ought to be spelt out—there may be partners who contribute funds but do not take part in day-to-day operations and those who handle the daily operations of the business. A general partnership assumes that profits, liability and management duties are divided equally among all partners. Think of a partnership as a pie with equal slices. For there to be equal distribution of profits, liability and duties, a Partnership Agreement executed by all partners must set out the proportion assigned to each partner.

The key characteristics of a General Partnership are:

A. Unlimited liability. In a general partnership, all partners are individually liable; hence, partners may be required to use personal assets to pay off debt if the partnership cannot meet its obligations.

B. Minimal tax filing is required. This category of businesses is assessed for tax under the Personal Income Tax Act (PITA) in the same manner as individuals/enterprise. In most countries, including Nigeria, Partners are assessed in their individual names, based on the share of partnership profits allocated to them. As a partnership is a creation of a federal law, it will be liable to remitting certain business tax to the Federal Government where it conducts business. It is paramount that a tax consultant is engaged from the onset to advise on the tax obligations of the entity, prior to settling on this legal structure.

C. Limited formal requirements. General partnerships are the easiest type of business structure to form because they require limited formal requirements or paperwork to exist. Because such partnerships are so easily created, you ought to choose your partners carefully and, as much as possible, enter into a partnership with a written document that guides the behaviour of all parties (Partnership Agreement).

2) Limited Liability Partnership (LLP)[1]

A Limited Liability Partnership combines the flexible structure of a general partnership with the benefits of a limited liability entity. An LLP is a type of Partnership that restricts the personal liability for the debts of the partnership to the General Partner alone, who in turn has a veto over management decisions while the limited partners have limited liability as agreed in the Partnership Agreement and limited input with management decisions of the partnership. These limits depend on the extent of each partner's investment proportion and is highly reliant on the partnership agreement between the partners.

A limited partnership must consist of at least one general partner, with others as limited partners.

The key characteristics of a Limited Partnership are:

A. The entity has a separate legal existence from members of the partnership. It has unlimited capacity and it can do anything that a natural person can do, including holding property, entering into contracts, suing and being sued.

B. The entity has a tax advantage, like a General Partnership, as it is not a recognized entity for companies' income tax purposes. It is treated for tax purposes as a partnership and the Members are taxed as partners, each being liable for tax on their share of the income or gains of the LLP.2 It is essential to engage the services of a tax consultant that can determine all tax obligations of the partnership in line with the business activities of the partnership.

C. In the event of winding up, the liability of the partners is limited to the amount that each partner has subscribed to under the terms of the registration document and/or the limited liability partnership agreement submitted to the Registrar. Note that there must be a general partner who will incur unlimited liability for the debts of the LLP. This means that the general partner's asset can be applied to offset the debts of the LLP.

D. It is a convenient vehicle for use as special purpose vehicles/entities [SPVs/SPEs] because it can be registered and dissolved without going through the elaborate process of winding up a company under the Companies and Allied Matters Act.

3) Limited Liability Company (LLC)

A Limited Liability Company is a private company owned by the members of the club, with each member recognized as a shareholder. An LLC may be:

A. Limited by shares, where the liability of each member is limited by the memorandum of association to the amount unpaid on the shares held by that shareholder.

B. Limited by guarantee, where the liability of members is limited by the memorandum to a monetary amount. The members may undertake to contribute to the assets of the company in the event of it being wound up.

C. Unlimited, where there is no limit on the liability of members.

The key characteristics of a Limited Liability Company are:

A. Limited liability. The shareholders are legally responsible for the company's debts only to the extent of the amount of capital they invested. They are not personally liable for any debt incurred by the company. As such, if the company faces loss under any circumstances, the personal assets of the shareholders are not at risk.

B. An LLC is required to file corporate tax returns to the relevant tax authority. They must prepare annual accounts i.e. statement of accounts, yearly which must be IFRS (international Financial Reporting Standard) compliant. It implies that a chartered accountant may be engaged to carry out this function on an annual basis. There is a minimum tax payable on an annual basis.

C. A private limited liability company cannot issue out its shares to the public. In addition, the transfer of its shares is restricted to members of the Company, therefore, when a member of a Private Limited Company desires to dispose his/her shares, the member can only transfer such shares to an existing member of the company or another individual, if the Company's Articles permit.

4) Co-operative Society

A co-operative society is an autonomous and voluntary association of individuals who come together with the objective of owning common property and promoting the economic interest of its members. A co-operative society may be registered as an industrial, primary, or secondary co-operative society.

An industrial co-operative society comprises at least six (6) persons and is required to provide evidence that it is commercially viable before it can be registered.

A primary co-operative society may be registered if it has at least ten (10) persons, each of whom must have attained the age of sixteen (16) years old, and all of whom must be resident in the state where the co-operative society will be operational.

A secondary co-operative society may be established and registered if it has at least five (5) registered co-operative societies as its prospective members.

The key characteristics of a Co-operative Society are:

A. **State control.** Co-operative societies are placed under state control through registration. While getting registered, a society must submit details about the members and the business it is to undertake. It must maintain books of accounts, which are to be audited by government auditors. A co-operative organization can be shut down if record keeping is found to be inaccurate or not regularly updated.

B. **Separate legal entity.** A co-operative society is registered under the Co-operative Societies Act. Once registered, a society becomes a separate legal entity with limited liability of its members. Death, insolvency or lunacy of a member does not affect the existence of a society. It can enter into agreements with others and can purchase or sell property in its own name.

C. **Exemption from tax.** The Companies Income Tax Act in Nigeria exempts co-operative societies from tax on the profits and gains from all trade or business a society engages in on behalf of its members. The entity is also exempted from stamp duties and value added tax.3

D. **Dissolution.** A co-operative society may by special resolution, authorize its own dissolution. The dissolution of a co-operative society by its members is called voluntary dissolution, while an involuntary dissolution occurs If a court rules to dissolve it and liquidate its assets.

The Legal Agreement

A legal agreement should be signed by all members of the club. in addition to getting registered as a legal entity. Executing a legal agreement is important for the following reasons:

1) It is a great way to outline legal guidelines for operational activities like opening a bank account, managing member contributions and financial accounts, receipt of external funds, making investment decisions, taking on new members and member exit provisions etc. Other key areas can be addressed in this document

2) The legal agreement will state clearly all terms that apply to formation and purpose of the investment club.

3) It also helps with seeking legal recourse if required.

Investment Club Registration Options

Entity	Liability	Tax	Registration requirement	Continuity
General Partnership (GP)	All partners have unlimited liability for all business transactions, debts and partners' share.	Assessed for tax under the Personal Income Tax Act (PITA) in the same manner as individuals/ enterprises. Partners are assessed in their individual names.	The easiest type of business structure to register because it requires limited paperwork to register	A General Partnership ceases to exist on the death or withdrawal of any partner
Limited Partnership (LP)	An LP restricts the personal liability for the debts of the partnership to the General Partner alone. Limited partners are limited by investment.	It is treated for tax purposes as a partnership and the Members are taxed as partners, each being liable for tax on their share of the income or gains of the LLP	At least one general partner is required to control the business for registration as a legal entity.	Partnership may be terminated on the exit of a general partner, unless legal agreement states a substitute to the general partner upon exit.
Limited Liability Company (LLC)	A private company owned by the members of the club, with each member recognized as a shareholder.	An LLC is required to file corporate tax returns to the relevant tax authority. They must prepare annual accounts which must be IFRS (International Financial Reporting Standard) compliant.	Must meet minimum shareholding requirement and be registered according to Corporate Affairs Commission (CAC) requirements Must have a Board of Directors.	An LLC stands as a legal entity and can survive member exits. On death of members, may continue to exist based on continuity clauses in legal agreement.
Co-operative society	A co-operative society is registered under the Co-operative Societies Act. Once registered, it becomes a separate legal entity with limited liability of its members	The Companies Income Tax Act in Nigeria exempts co-operative societies from tax on the profits and gains from all trade or business it engages in on behalf of its members.	Co-operative societies are under state control are therefore registered based on individual state laws.	Death, insolvency or lunacy of a member does not affect the continued existence of a co-operative society. A co-operative society may by special resolution, authorize its own dissolution.

Choice of Legal registration

Honestly, one of the mistakes I think my investment club made when we got started was registering our investment club as a limited liability company. That's because a limited liability company is required to file Value Added Tax (VAT) monthly and this responsibility has become a burden.

We do not operate a regular business and some of our investments are long term in nature, yet we are mandated to report future earnings to the tax authority. Do not get me wrong, we support the local tax authority; however, we did not need that extra responsibility. While my investment club is not registered as a limited liability partnership, I suggest you consider this option, so you don't get into activities that are not relevant to the goal of your investment club.

Legal agreement

All my investment club had at inception was a two-page guideline I came up with. It was not reviewed by a legal counsel or any expert. However, once we started making investment decisions, it was clear we needed something more elaborate.

Review my legal agreement checklist and make sure you execute an agreement with members of your club. This activity ensures you discuss and agree on pertinent issues that may come up in future.

Money Talk

Regular contributions are a key characteristic of a financial investment club. One important decision your club will make is the monetary amount each member will contribute and how frequently the contributions will occur.

It is important that regular monetary contributions, both in terms of the amount and frequency, are set at a convenient level for all members. A convenient contribution will help the club avoid repeated cases of default so that you can make investments decisions according to plan. You may also consider setting a lower threshold for everyone at inception, and slowly ramping up after a while.

The clubs in my network make monthly contributions to match the monthly pay schedule common in Nigeria. Other contribution cycles to consider include quarterly or annual contributions.

Another thing to consider is a lock-up period for contributions. A lock-up period is the period when the collated financial contribution is invested, and income earned from what is invested is ploughed back towards building the club funds. During this period, cash is not paid out to any member of the club in any form, save for operational expenses.

The lock-up period will discourage repeated pay-outs or exits that may inhibit the growth of the fund. All members can agree to contribute 'X' monthly/quarterly/annually for a defined period (long-term/medium term). A medium-term period can be defined as a five-year period, and long-term period as any period longer than five (5) years.

When You Don't Get the Bank Notification

Does this really happen? Yes, it does.

Isn't it awkward when a member misses a contribution payment? You're right on the money. It is. This is why you need guidelines to guide the club in making decisions if or when it happens.

All members should be encouraged to avoid defaulting on monetary contributions. One of the ways to avoid a default situation is ensuring you all agree on a payment amount that is convenient for every member from inception. You may also set up a system to send gentle reminders early in the payment cycle to prevent potential default.

While a payment default by any member is a situation you want to avoid as a club, in the event it does happen, guidelines will help the club to manage the situation appropriately.

Guidelines for defaults should be agreed upon, put in place, and communicated to every member of the club. These guidelines should also be stated in the partnership/shareholders' agreement before the club commences operations, so that all members are aware before they join the investment club.

Sample guidelines for payment default

You may consider the following penalties for payment defaults:

I. A warning on the first default on a contribution.

II. A 10% - 20% interest payment on total contribution owed after two (2) months of default.

III. A 20% - 30% interest payment on total contribution owed after three (3) months of default.

IV. If a member of the club still owes accumulated contribution for four (4) months, by the fourth month, that member should be advised to withdraw from the investment club.

V. Dividend or interest benefits may be withheld from defaulting member.

These are all the ways my investment club and some of the other clubs in my network manage default situations.

I acknowledge there might be special circumstances where a member of the club defaults on payment due to reasons beyond their control. If this occurs, the other members of the club need to decide if the circumstances are reasonable enough to lead to a default or not. If all members agree that the circumstances should not lead to a default, a decision should be made on if/what penalty will apply to the defaulting member.

Members do not need to contribute the same amount of money to the club. Each member can be allocated shares of the legal entity per the capital contributions made by that member. We didn't try this option in my club, but I think it is an option that can be explored to accommodate different financial capabilities in the members.

It is important to set a date deadline for remitting club contributions. Common dates are the 25th or 30th of every month. Each member should be encouraged to transfer their contribution to the corporate bank account opened specifically for the club. This means the investment club needs to be legally registered and the corporate bank account opened and operational before contributions commence.
(more on bank accounts and signatories in chapter 4)

All members should automate payment by setting up a standing instruction on personal bank accounts to ensure contributions are transferred by the end of every month without delay.

During the lifetime of the investment club, member contributions may increase or decrease as the club wishes. Once all members of the club agree on a monetary contribution, it should remain valid for a minimum period of 1 year. This is advised to get all members settled and used to contributing that amount monthly. Members may review monetary contributions and re-validate or agree on a new monthly contribution on an annual basis.

Finally, you should add a clause to your legal agreement and contribution framework that allows for member exits only after the first six months of the club's existence.

Disclaimer - The section on legal structure is for information purposes only and should not be construed as professional legal advice about which structure is best for your investment club.

Summary of Key Points

Key Questions:

1) What are the four (4) important areas my partners and I need to decide on before we start our investment club?
2) Do we need to register our club as a legal entity?
3) How do we manage awkward situations like member exits and payment defaults?

How do you find the right members for your club?
A. Find people who are willing to contribute to the success of your club and not simply be club members.
B. It is better to start with people who share similar values when it comes to making essential money and investment decisions.
C. The ideal number of members for your investment club is five (5) members at a minimum and 12 members at a maximum. With 5 members, you can pool sizeable capital to invest, and at a maximum of 12 members, you can avoid being ineffective.

Why did you decide to set up an investment club?
A. Work with the members of your club to discuss comprehensively and agree on a core investment goal or objective for the club.
B. Discuss options on how long the investment club will exist, when or if you will make dividend payments, and what type of investment options you prefer to invest in.
C. This step is the core foundation for your club and it may mar future investment decisions if not discussed comprehensively and settled.

On election of new members and managing exits
A. Define guidelines to manage these events when they occur.
   The guidelines should include requirements for new members and an exit process for members who wish to withdraw their membership.
B. Work on making unanimous decisions as a club.

The Legal framework

A. Consider all the pros and cons of the options available for you to register your investment club as a legal entity and decide on an option that works best.

B. Execute a legal agreement to protect your interest individually and as a club.

Managing financial contribution

A. In a financial investment club, all members make contributions to the club's fund and agree on an amount that is convenient for each member to contribute on a regular basis.

B. Set up penalties to manage default on contributions.

Worksheet – Action Steps for Starting Your Investment Club

Name of Investment Club _____

Legal structure	
Number of members	

Contributions

- Routine _____
- Fixed term before pay-outs_____(Investment tenor for the club)
- Agreed date for contributions _____

Legal agreement checklist

This checklist will ensure you capture all the relevant legal considerations in your legal agreement

Tenor of investment club

Purpose of your investment club	
Capital contributions (Amount, payment cycle, etc.)	
Managing operational activities of the club (club meetings, etc.)	
Managing books of account	
Terms for making investment decisions	
Terms/penalties for payment default	
Club roles and responsibilities	
Requirements for new members	
Terms for transfer of membership shares	
Terms for membership withdrawal and payment	
Dispute resolution	
Terms of exit	

"Begin with
the end in mind."
- *Stephen Covey*

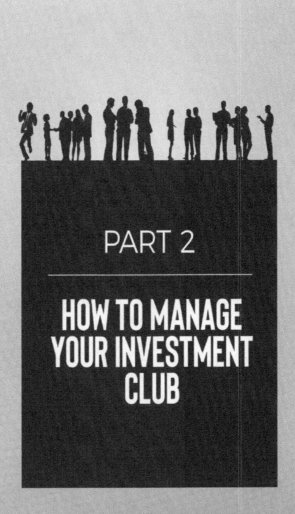

PART 2

HOW TO MANAGE YOUR INVESTMENT CLUB

The Investment Club Framework ™

Leveraging resources to build wealth together, spread risks,
gain rewards and make an impact on society.

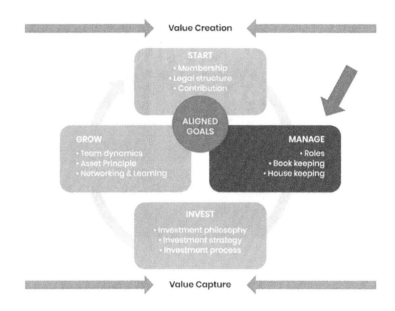

4

GROUP EFFORT, NOT INDIVIDUAL EFFORT

"No one can whistle a symphony.
It takes a whole orchestra to play it."
-H.E. Luccock

I got introduced to the concept of teamwork quite early in life. When you have five siblings and you need to do household chores, you see the need for everyone to play active roles daily. My siblings and I had to be assigned chores, so that one person didn't end up doing all the work just because they were hardworking. Growing up with five siblings also taught me that once everyone pitches in to get the chores done, you get less cranky parents and more time to play or watch TV on a weekend.

During my MBA program, I appreciated teamwork even more. There is so much value to be gained when all members pitch in to contribute time, knowledge and skills to a project. We were more likely to ace a project when everyone pitched in.

It was easy for me to take on a lot of responsibility in my investment club because I was passionate about making it work, but I saw the folly in this approach soon enough when I became too busy with other pressing responsibilities. We work in teams in almost every area of our lives—in marriage, at work, in school, and with friends. It is important to work as a team in an investment club as well.

Yes, Mr. President

Every member of the club needs to play an active role in managing club affairs. Nobody wants to be a member of a club where only one or two members bear the workload. That's enough to demotivate anyone any day.

Functional roles can be assigned to each member of the club based on individual strength and area of expertise. This will provide every member the opportunity to add value to the club in core areas where they have clear strengths.

Sample roles[1] include:

I. **Club President** - This person takes a leadership role and ensures the club implements the agreed investment strategy. The President presides over meetings and is given the authority to set the club's schedule.

II. **Vice President** - This person acts as a stand-in when the President is absent.

III. **Club Treasurer** - This person manages the club finances. The Treasurer monitors member contributions and investment positions of the club—unrealized losses/gains, liquidity positions, etc. The Treasurer also prepares financial reports that are to be distributed to members periodically. This role requires a detail-oriented individual who is comfortable with numbers.

IV. **Club Secretary** - This role manages the administrative tasks of the club. It includes managing the club's bank accounts and filing returns and any other regulatory filings. The Club Secretary is also in charge of keeping the minutes of all meetings.

Other roles your club can consider include:

I. **A Research Analyst** to collate and present all material related to investment opportunities in the pipeline. This person will also keep track of the selection process for individual opportunities.

II.   A **Brand/Marketing Specialist** to manage the club's strategic brand and positioning. Responsibilities will include creating a logo, website, and social media handles; liaising with the investment club network; and keeping all the members informed of social activities to attend.

A Second Look at Assigning Roles

You might experience some difficulty assigning roles in your investment club. That difficulty could arise if members prove unwilling to take instructions from their peers. It could also arise if some members take on all the responsibility, leaving others to feel they do not need to get involved.

What if you decide to see your investment club as an organization that needs structure, and your friends as partners in making your organization successful? Would that change your mind about being led by friends? What if you stood the risk of losing all your records because only one member manages the club records and there are no backup records? Or what if you stood the risk of losing your money because one member made a clearly biased investment decision? Would that change your mind about taking on an active role?

It changed the way one of the clubs in my network operated. After a series of bad investment decisions, they knew it was time to stop leaving the investment decisions to one member. You do not need to wait for that to happen. Start with a good understanding of each member's strengths, and assign responsibilities based on strength, expertise and willingness to do the work required.

Finally, avoid imposing roles on members. Some roles can be shared if two members feel they can carry out that role. The truth is you might not need all the roles filled at the inception of your club. Some of these roles are simply "nice-to-haves" which you may not require till much later.

Keep the Rats Away

We all need a little housekeeping from time to time. It is important to keep your club operations running smoothly. Sample housekeeping guidelines include the following:

I. **Regular meetings** - Meet regularly to discuss research, investment prospects/decisions, and other matters of the club. Regular meetings can be monthly or quarterly. The presiding member may call special meetings at any time. You may also keep a virtual group for continuous real-time discussions. WhatsApp is a great tool for virtual groups.
    (See sample meeting agenda)

II. **Quorum for decisions** - A defined number of members should form a quorum for making decisions. This is very important to manage disagreements within the club. For instance, in a club with 6 members, they can agree to accept a decision once at least four members agree to that decision.

III. **Club financial statements** - Agree on a routine/schedule for sending out financial statements to all the club members. This is necessary to keep every member duly informed.

IV. **Bank account signatories** - Open a corporate bank account and appoint members who are readily available as signatories of the club's bank account. For security reasons, it is best to designate this role to the presiding member and treasurer. These roles can also be rotated amongst members on an annual or bi-annual basis.

Not Fun, But Necessary

For most of us, keeping financial records is a boring aspect of managing the affairs of an investment club, but it is necessary from inception. It is necessary because you need to keep track of your investment portfolio's growth. You also need to keep proper records to satisfy all regulatory requirements such as tax filings.

Keep your accounting records as simple as possible, so it does not become a burden. Keep it simple until you can afford to outsource it.

All accounting is based on a simple equation:

Assets = Liabilities + Owner's Equity

In simple terms, assets are what you own, liabilities are what you owe, and owner's equity is what you can take out theoretically as a shareholder. In an investment club, you start out with no liabilities, so your club accounting will show records of what you own in terms of assets and what each member's share of the asset is.

Assets = Owner's Equity.

Assets

Your assets include cash (money market securities), and investment in different asset categories (stock, mutual funds, real estate, private equity). The value of the club's assets is also known as the net asset value of the club.

Your club's assets will increase as you receive dividends on your stock portfolio, interest on securities, rental income on real estate, or see the value of an asset increase. The club's value will also increase as members continue to make monetary contributions.

The value of your club's assets will decrease with pay-outs on expenses, member exits or withdrawals, and depreciation of portfolio assets.

Owner's Equity

The second part of the accounting equation is where you keep track of ownership details. Some of the key things to consider here are:

    I. How much you earn from investments in the club.

    II. How much of the club earnings should be taxed, paid out or ploughed back as capital.

In an investment club, members do not own a specific percentage of individual assets in the club. They own a percentage of the total assets of the club. Club ownership can be accounted for by using either a shareholding structure or unit-based ownership.

1) A Shareholding Structure

This is straightforward. The members own shares in the company. For instance, if an investment club is registered with 1m shares and has 5 members, each member owns one-fifth (20%) of the total value of shares. The shareholding structure also works where members do not make equal monetary contributions. However, once the shareholding structure reflects different monetary contributions at inception, that structure will have to be maintained throughout the duration of the club

2) Unit Based Ownership

This is different and accommodates flexible monetary contributions. With unit-based ownership, an investment club has the flexibility to assign ownership units to its members based on their monetary contribution. This structure assumes that further contributions, by each member, may not be equal at each contribution point.

Any time a member contributes to a unit-based investment club, that member purchases units. The number of units owned by each member may differ based on their contributions. If a member decides to take some money out, they redeem units. If a member decides to exit, the value of each unit may be valued at current market prices or at an agreed cost between two parties if another member decides to sell or redeem units. A member's ownership stake at any time is the value of that individual's member units divided by the total units managed by the investment club.

Keeping the Books

An investment club is under no stringent requirement to keep financial records in a specified format. However, if the club plans to invest in assets that require a presentation of financial records, it is best to ensure all records are kept in accordance with basic accounting reporting standards such as the IFRS (International

Financial Reporting Standard). Some guidelines to note include the following:

I.   The Club Treasurer should ensure records of all income, expenses, and investments are kept in detail. A basic Excel sheet can serve this purpose at the initial stage of the investment club. You can evolve into using a mobile application that provides this service.
II.   Records should be sent out to all members of the club on a quarterly/monthly basis, or as agreed by all members of the club. The minimum content of the periodic report should have been agreed by all members at inception.
III. Keep a receipt or invoice for every transaction.
IV. Ensure bank statements or stock brokerage accounts are reconciled with records on a monthly or quarterly basis. To keep reconciliation activities simple, an investment club should operate no more than three (3) bank accounts.
V.   Your assets should be valued, at minimum, on a quarterly basis. If the club has a stock portfolio, the portfolio can be valued monthly. As an investment club, you may consider carrying out fund valuations on a regular basis. This is important to track the growth of your fund's value.
VI. In addition, you should plan to get your financial statements audited on an annual basis. You may employ an external party to audit club financials and double check to ensure there are no errors in your records.

Please remember, investment clubs are about learning to make investment decisions and not about learning accounting, so keep it simple until you need to outsource it to be managed or valued by an external party.

Summary of Key Points

Key Questions:
1) How do we set up active roles in our club?
2) What kind of rules should guide housekeeping?
3) How do we keep proper records?

How do we assign roles in an investment club?
A. Assign functional roles based on each member's strength or preference.
B. Sample roles include a presiding member (President), a member who manages the funds (Club treasurer), and a member who manages operational tasks (Club Secretary).

Housekeeping, everyone?
A. Hold regular meetings to discuss investment options and other operational tasks.
B. Encourage on-going discussions and engagement in virtual groups. WhatsApp is a great tool for this.
C. Define a quorum for easier decision-making.
D. Prepare basic financial reports on a regular schedule.
E. Open a bank account and request for bank statements regularly.

How do we keep proper financial records?
A. You can keep the club's records in a basic Excel sheet or on money management mobile applications
B. You are under no stringent requirements to keep financial records in a specified format; however, be aware of regulatory accounting reporting formats so you can do this when required.
C. Keep all documents safe.
D. Carry out a fund valuation, at minimum, on an annual basis.

Worksheet: Action Steps for Managing Your Investment Club

Assigning Roles

Role	Name of member
e.g. Presiding member	

Housekeeping -Meeting Schedule

Type of meeting	Schedule
Investment team meeting	
Club meetings	
Annual meetings	

Financial statement schedule

Type of financial statement	Schedule
Annual statement	
Investment portfolio statement	

How many members form a quorum? _____

Corporate bank accounts

Type of account	Bank/ Institution	Signatories

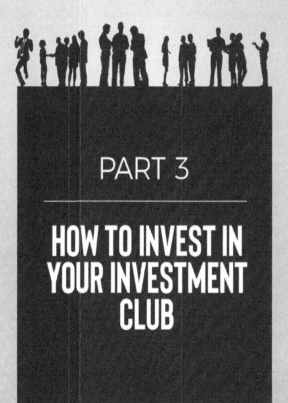

PART 3

HOW TO INVEST IN YOUR INVESTMENT CLUB

The Investment Club Framework ™

Leveraging resources to build wealth together, spread risks,
gain rewards and make an impact on society.

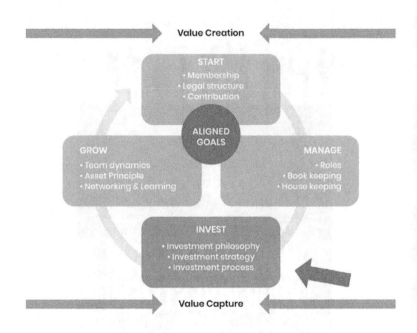

5
THIS IS WHAT
WE CAME TO DO

"Follow the money."
- *Peter Thiel*

It felt like a rush of adrenaline. We were giddy with excitement. It was our first investment as a club and it felt like this was what we came to do. Everything had led up to that point. Or so we thought.

We held meetings, had discussions, and thought about the risks associated with our investment decision. We believed we had all the risks covered and decided to go ahead and invest.

Mr. Oti was soft-spoken and seemed like a good businessman. He was in the transportation business. The kind of person you could trust to take you on a trip across town.

"I see an opportunity to meet the transport needs of young professionals who neither want to drive in traffic nor own cars. All they want is a vehicle and driver to pick them up from home, drop them off at the office, and repeat the cycle at the close of business," he said.

He had our attention.

"How long have you done this?" We asked. "A couple of months," he replied. "I decided to focus on serving this target market after I got a lot of requests for the same service. It offered a regular and more predictable income than waiting to get a call from a former client or waiting to be stopped while driving."

We had just finished our MBA program. We were his target market. We understood the needs of this market and thought it was a viable business opportunity. So, we asked what an investment would entail. Mr. Oti requested we purchase a minivan and agree on a lease-to-own contract over a two-year period.

This was where we made our first mistake.

When you lack an investment philosophy, any investment opportunity that promises good returns will seem viable even when it is not.

The Philosophy of Investments

Philosophy is not picking and choosing a body of thought based on personal
preferences or feelings. Philosophy is a pursuit. One can choose to be
philosophical. One can choose to be a philosopher.

Philosophy is a form of thinking meant to guide action or prescribe a way of life. The philosophic way of life, if there is one, is displayed in a life where action is best directed with the help of a clear philosophical trajectory.

In the same way, **an investment philosophy** is a coherent way of thinking about investment opportunities, how they work, and the types of mistakes you believe consistently underlie investor behaviour.[1] An investment philosophy is a set of core beliefs by every member of the club that, when harnessed, will drive the club's investment decisions.

It is important for the investment club's overall investment philosophy to align with the investment objective of each member of the club. For instance, if the club's investment objective is to build wealth by investing in a certain asset class, all members need to agree on this from inception. They also need to create guidelines that will help them make the final investment decision.

Factors such as monetary contribution, risk tolerance, time horizon, and liquidity needs should also be taken into consideration when deliberating on the investment objectives for the club.

We thought we had an investment objective—build wealth by investing in small businesses and other identified asset classes. That was not good enough, as we soon learnt. It was not enough to identify an investment opportunity. You also need to test the opportunity for scale and future opportunities for growth.

Think Uber. The business model for Uber has an inbuilt strategy for scale and rapid growth across the globe. Mr. Oti had no such strategy. In retrospect, it seemed like all he wanted was an additional car to own in two years. One of the actions that consistently underlies bad investment decisions is the refusal to consider a business' potential to grow, scale up operations, and make a significant impact on society. I do not believe you can make an impact on society by thinking small.

Your core beliefs should be reflected in your investment strategy and reviewed regularly to generate new strategies when old strategies do not work.

10 Questions to Help Define Your Investment Philosophy

1. What are your core investment beliefs?
2. Do you understand your philosophy and why you believe in it?
3. Do you know the potential risks?
4. Does it suit your personality and individual circumstances?
5. Will your philosophy help you follow whatever strategy you implement?
6. What constraints are necessary for turning your philosophy into a portfolio?
7. What will you own and why will you own it?
8. What will cause you to buy or sell?
9. What will cause you to make changes to your portfolio over time?
10. What types of investments or strategies will you avoid?

Culled from www.awealthofcommonsense.com

Once you identify your core beliefs, the next step is to put together an investment strategy. **An investment strategy** puts your investment philosophy into practice. An investment strategy is a set of rules, behaviours, or procedures designed to guide the club's selection of an investment portfolio. Your strategy should consider factors such as economic trends, political climate, inflation, and interest rates. Other factors include risk tolerance levels and short-term or long-term growth objectives.

Your investment strategy should outline your decisions on the following:

I.   Asset class(es).
II.   Preferred industries in which you wish to invest.

III.   Size of investment—minimum and maximum amount that can be invested together with a specification of portfolio mix or diversity, if any.
IV.   Minimum Return on Investment (ROI) expected on each investment.
V.   Stage of company—seed, start-up, or growth stage.
VI.   Profile of management team of the company.

After a while, you will discover that mapping out an investment strategy is the easy part. Sticking with the strategy is what separates investors from speculators. In your investment club, make it a priority to have a laser focus on a consistent long-term strategy through steady purchase of well-diversified investments.

Example 1[2]
Belief: Start-up businesses are high risk investments.
Investment Philosophy: Start-up businesses are high risk investments compared to businesses that have existed for at least 5 years.
Investment Strategy:
   I. Invest only in businesses that have existed for at least five (5) years.
   II. Invest only in businesses that show healthy cash flow over a two to three-year period.

Example 2
Belief: We should not put all our eggs in one basket.
Investment Philosophy: Investing in one asset class will expose us to risk.
Investment Strategy:

I. At no point will we invest more than 50% of our funds in any investment.
II. Minimum ROI for high risk investments will be 20-25%

Example 3

Belief: We should avoid making poor judgement calls on investment decisions.

Investment Philosophy: When a member of the club is emotionally connected to an investment opportunity, we might make a poor judgement call.

Investment Strategy:

I. We will not invest in any opportunity where a member of the club has a family or emotional connection.

An investment club may have as many investment philosophies as it deems necessary. Just ensure you review your philosophies on a regular basis to check for relevance in current economic conditions or the club's vision. Investment philosophies can also be changed once they have been tested and found to be unnecessary or no longer relevant.

Why Do We Need Investment Philosophies and Strategies?[8]

I. If you lack a core set of beliefs, you will be easy prey for dishonest businessmen or unprofitable business opportunities, with each one claiming to provide the best returns in the market.[3]

II. Switching from strategy to strategy might cause you to keep changing your asset portfolio. This may affect the club's earnings adversely.

III. If a philosophy is not agreed upon at inception, you might end up inadvertently employing a strategy that goes against your club's objectives, risk aversion tactics, and personal characteristics of members. This will result in disagreements and negative nuances in your club affairs.

What Asset Classes Do We Invest In?

Let's start with defining what an asset class is. An asset class is a group of investments that have similar characteristics, behave similarly, and are subject to similar market forces, laws and regulations. There are four major asset classes defined in this book. They are equity, debt, cash, and alternative investments.

1) **Equity**

Equity provides ownership interest to an investor. You can either purchase equity publicly on the stock exchange or privately (private equity).

A. **Public Equity**

I. Equities (also known as 'ordinary shares' or 'shares') are issued by a public limited company and are traded on the stock market. When you invest in an equity, you buy a share in a company and become a shareholder.

II. Public equity or stock can be broken down either by industry e.g. manufacturing, automotive, or energy — or by a more general characteristic of the investment e.g. value, growth, or blue chip.

III. A value stock is a stock that is low-priced relative to its estimated true worth using either earnings, dividends, or book value as a basis for estimation. On the other hand, a growth stock is may be expensive relative to the business' current earnings; however, investors think the price is justified by its high potential for future growth in earnings.

IV. If members of your club are not savvy with handpicking publicly quoted stock, they can start with investing in mutual funds or seek the advice of stock analysts before investing in the stock market.

Pros of Investing in Public Equity (Stock Market)

I. You can purchase stock easily by giving your stockbroker or financial planner an instruction to purchase on your behalf.

II. When you invest in the stock market, you gain access to diverse companies in different sectors of the economy, which you can leverage on for growth in your investment portfolio.

III.   Some stocks provide income in the form of dividends. Dividend payment can help you grow your investment portfolio.
IV.   It is a liquid investment. This means if you need cash for an immediate opportunity, you can give an instruction to sell and exit.

Cons of Investing in Public Equity (Stock Market)

I.   The Stock Market can be very volatile. You can lose significant value in your investment if a company performs poorly or you bought a good company at the wrong time say at the peak of the market.
II.   As an ordinary shareholder, you stand the risk of getting paid last if the company goes into liquidation. Preferred shareholders are paid first.
III.   There is no guaranteed return on stock investments. Shareholders make returns that is directly related to the fortunes of the underlying business. With the possibility of high returns comes the possibility of losing money.

Key Points to Note Before You Invest in Public Equity

I.   The most important consideration for investing in a good stock is the future earnings potential of the company. An investor should review financial statements of a company before they make a decision to invest and also take into account the economic outlook of the country and specific industry the company operates in.

II. The Stock Market works in cycles and if you are beginner investors, it is important to work with professionals who can provide analytical research and recommendations. Don't invest on a whim or fad.

III. When you invest in a company, you are investing in the company's management team and products/services. The quality of the company's management team and nature of the product/services the company offers has a direct effect on the performance of that company's stock.

B. **Private Equity**

I. Private equity is equity capital invested in operating companies not quoted on a public stock exchange (market).

II. Private equity investment can be done through three diverse strategies:

i) Venture capital investments in typically early-stage or even start-up firms that emphasize revenue growth and have a specific focus in rapidly growing industries.4

ii) Leveraged buyouts (LBOs) where well-established and publicly-traded companies are acquired and converted to private ownership using debt.5

iii) Investing in a private equity fund professionally managed by a private fund manager who has a strong track record and provides sufficient transparency.

Pros of investing in Private Equity
  I. Private equity provides access to new opportunities. It may be difficult to make new discoveries on the public stock exchange. Private companies provide hidden value that can be invested in and nurtured to grow significantly.
  II. When you invest in a public company, your role is generally passive. However, you can take a more active role in the private company in which you invest. An active role provides the opportunity to ensure the company acts in the investor's interest.

Cons of investing in Private Equity
  I. It is not a very liquid investment option. Funds invested in a private company may not be accessible for years. You may also be at the mercy of the company and other shareholders if you want to purchase additional shares or sell down.
  II. You may not get access to data to analyse how the company is performing before investing unless you are an insider.
  III. The likelihood of the success of a private equity investment depends on multiple factors: management, growth potential realized, exit environment, etc. Do not invest what you cannot afford to lose. A due diligence exercise is important before you invest.

Key points to note for Private Equity

I. Always negotiate the value of the equity offered for sale based on the company's estimated cash flow and growth capacity before you make an investment decision.

II. If both parties do not agree on the value of company's equity, you can consider offering an initial convertible note. A convertible note is an investment vehicle often used by start-up seed investors who wish to delay establishing a valuation until a later round of funding or milestone. Convertible notes are structured as debt with the intention of converting the debt to equity or cash at an agreed milestone.

III. A convertible provides the opportunity to decide if the start-up captures enough value that might end up becoming valuable to the club as shareholders. The convertible note may or may not be converted to equity at the club's request.

IV. Should you decide to do a convertible note, then assess the investment the same way you would assess a debt (fixed income) investment. See below.

2) Debt (Fixed Income)

I. This involves lending money to a corporate organization or government at an interest rate. Debt provides financial interest to an investor.

II. Fixed income securities are issued by companies and governments as a way of raising money.

III. Some examples of fixed income securities include government bonds, corporate bonds, other types of bonds, and certificates of deposit.

IV. Fixed income securities are generally considered to offer stable returns, have lower risk than equities—and therefore deliver lower returns than equities.

V. Different financial institutions offer different rates on fixed income securities, so it's best to carry out a competitive check on rates before you make an investment decision.

3) Cash or Cash Equivalent

I. This is the money in your bank account.

II. Cash equivalent is an asset class that can be easily converted into cash or is cash itself. They are short-term in nature, e.g. investments in deposits or treasury bills, and have a holding period of less than one year.

III. Examples of cash equivalents include bank fixed deposits, savings account, current account, short-term treasury bills, loans, and money market funds (a pooled investment with the above possible investments).

IV. Cash equivalents allow you, an investor, to invest money in assets that generate some returns, or reduce the risk of erosion or deflation of value.

V. It is important to note that there is an opportunity cost to holding cash. That cost is the return that investor could have earned by investing the cash in a new product or expanding business.

4) Alternative Investments

I. This asset class puts together all the assets not included in the conventional asset classes — equity, debt, and cash.

II. Alternative investments include real estate, commodities, venture capital funds, hedge funds, etc.

III. Interested in real estate? Work with a credible real estate firm to establish the credibility of a land/property purchase before you make the final investment decision. It will save you stress, hassle, and/or loss.

IV. Small and Medium Enterprises (SMEs) are also included in this category. Key things to consider for this option is not to be easily sold on a business idea — check out the business plan (if the business has not started operations), check out the financials (if the business has been in operation for a while), calculate your downside risk and don't invest money you cannot afford to lose (Read more on this in the case study section).

The Investment Management Process

The investment management process requires adequate planning, execution and monitoring for all decisions. Planning involves agreeing on investment objectives, philosophy, and strategy. These can be collated into a policy document for every member to review and approve.

Execution requires making critical decisions about asset categories in which to invest and assigning weights to each category in the portfolio. These decisions will inform the implementation plan.

Subsequent monitoring is required to evaluate the performance of the assets in the club's portfolio on a regular basis. Different asset categories require different monitoring schedules; however, for the sake of consistency, review of investment performance should be scheduled at least once a month. Investment performance should be evaluated based on agreed performance benchmarks.

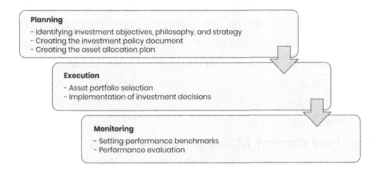

Planning
- Identifying investment objectives, philosophy, and strategy
- Creating the investment policy document
- Creating the asset allocation plan

Execution
- Asset portfolio selection
- Implementation of investment decisions

Monitoring
- Setting performance benchmarks
- Performance evaluation

Understanding Asset Allocation

Asset allocation involves allocating your club's funds to different asset classes such as equity, debt, alternative investments, or cash. The process of determining what mix of assets to hold in your portfolio should be well thought out.

Your investment club's ideal asset mix will depend largely on your investment strategy and risk appetite. However, note that a portfolio that only contains one or two asset classes is not diversified and may not be prepared to take advantage of all the swings the financial markets may throw at you.

1) The best Investment Strategy is to keep a Diversified Portfolio.

This simply means you should have a healthy mix of asset classes in your club's portfolio. Research shows that it is the best way to gain the highest return at the lowest risk over time. Financial planners suggest that you always adjust your asset allocation in response to changes in the business cycle and your financial goals. For instance, if you allocated 50% of your portfolio to investing in the stock market, when an economic turn changes the value of the stock in your portfolio to 40% of your portfolio, you should adjust your portfolio accordingly if you intend to retain the previous asset allocation.

2) Risk vs. Reward

If members are risk averse or conservative, they should take measured risks with adequate expert advice. If members are risk takers, they can choose to invest in high-risk investment opportunities. Balance and diversification is always advised. Typically, low levels of uncertainty (low-risk) are associated with low potential returns, whereas high levels of uncertainty (high-risk) are associated with high potential returns.

3) Making Investment Decisions

Every investment decision should be made based on the general investment philosophy and investment strategies of the club. Arbitrary decisions and measures are best avoided.

There's a lot to learn about investing. Don't get overwhelmed if you feel it's a bit difficult to figure out. Reach out to experts in the various asset fields and seek advice. One of the ways your investment club can approach investing is to pick an asset class at a time. Learn all you can and start investing before you take on another asset class.

How to Manage Your Investment Portfolio

Investing and managing the club's portfolio will require substantial commitment upfront. The club may decide to engage the services of an investment professional to develop a strategy or choose an investment approach. The decision to hire a third party should be taken with full disclosure on the cost required to manage the funds continuously or just at the onset.

Key Points to Note with Managing Your Investment Portfolio

I. Focus on building a well-balanced investment portfolio based on stated investment objectives. A well-balanced investment portfolio will protect your portfolio from the inevitable ups and downs over time.

II. Once all club members agree on an investment portfolio, have a provision to review the investment portfolio on an annual basis, to ensure the investment mix remains aligned with the club's investment objectives. Sticking with your investment strategy does not mean ignoring your investments. Financial advisors suggest revisiting your asset allocation—the combination of stocks, bonds, private equity and money market/stable value investments in your account—at least once a year to see if the club's portfolio needs to be rebalanced.

III. Over time, the rise and fall of markets may change your asset allocation, thereby changing your investment mix. For instance, the club's initial investment portfolio may have included the following: 20% in public equity, 30% in debt, 20% in private equity, and 30% in money market/stable value investments. If the value of your private equity investment declines, your overall portfolio allocation might shift to 20% in public equity, 40% in bonds, 5% in private equity and 35% in money market/stable value investments. Changing your portfolio mix simply means adjusting the asset allocation to specific asset classes to restore the initial investment mix. This is also known as rebalancing

IV. Try not to get emotional about your investment decisions. If the members of the club cannot stomach market volatility, the club may not have the temperament to manage its own portfolio.

Investment Case Studies

Case Study 1 – Cargot Ltd

Cargot Ltd.* operates in the ecommerce space. The company started operations barely 6 months before initial

> **Tomie's Advice on Investment Decisions**
>
> My experience has taught me that each investment asset class is a deep end that needs to be explored and understood in entirety. When we started our investment club, we thought we could invest in every asset class if it was profitable but, boy, were we wrong. My advice? Define a maximum of two asset classes in which you can build capacity and invest in at inception. Once you build capacity in these asset classes, you may decide to invest in another asset class entirely or stick to only one asset class.
>
> This is best practice. The National Association of Investment Clubs (NAIC) invests strictly in the stock market and they have done this for over 50 years. As a result, all the members have built proficiency and a good understanding of investing in the markets.
>
> Also, seek out objective experts who can guide your club on investing in a specific asset class and help you deepen your knowledge in that asset class.
>
> Finally, there will always be the risk of losing money, so you should expect a degree of risk with every investment opportunity and every investment decision. It is important for you to explicitly define your risk profile, plan to mitigate risk, and ensure your decisions are reflected in the agreed investment strategy.

contact with the investment club. The Nigerian ecommerce industry is an emerging one with several strong players and some small players. Cargot had an interesting business model that sought to help the company carve out a niche in the ecommerce space. This business model provided healthy average margins at 25% - 30% on each retail transaction.

We decided not to invest directly in equity for two reasons. First, we did not trust the valuation figures. Many start-up companies usually have optimistic valuation figures based on unproven growth indices. Secondly, we wanted to give the management a chance to demonstrate it could really manage and build the business sustainably.

Subsequently, we provided a working capital loan on the premise that we would decide to invest more funds if we saw sustainable traction in revenues and overall business. Eventually, we did not invest more funds, and these were my lessons:

I. Investing in start-ups is risky and involves more resources, including time and professional advice to management on strategy and operations.
II. In early stage investing, focus more on the skills and abilities of the founder(s)/management team.
III. When in doubt, give out a loan (debt instrument). It reduces the risk of investing in equity. Exiting a start-up might be tough in the local market scene as the start-up environment is still emerging with few long-term investors.

Case Study 2- Beantrip Ltd

Beantrip Ltd.* had been in operations for four years in the local agriculture sector. The company's founders purchased an old company to jump-start business and operational activities in the oil palm processing sector. Struggling with keeping the company afloat, they sought funding from individual investors in the first three years of operations. Eventually, the company achieved some level of stability in its fourth year and needed additional funds to expand its operations.

We received a proposal from one of Beantrip's directors to raise capital from us. We thought the proposal looked interesting and the company had a lot of potential; however, we needed more information about the company's numbers. We made a request for additional information and received feedback that the company had been subsidized by one of the founders for several years so the financial records they had did not provide a correct picture of the company's operations.

We had two choices—to invest, or not to invest because they could not provide comprehensive financial records.

We decided to invest because:

I. One of the company's founders had a good reputation and pedigree. At the end of the day, this was the most important reason we invested in this company.

II. The company operated in a sector with very few players who were currently not meeting the local demand gap.

III. The sector had huge potential and we wanted to be part of a great African story.

IV. We mitigated the risk by offering a convertible loan with annual coupon payments for two years, after which we had the option to convert to equity.

Over time, this investment turned out to be one of our best investment decisions as an investment club. The key lesson here is that, sometimes, you might need to make an investment decision based on the pedigree of company's management team and take the risk anyway. However, if all the members of your investment club vote unanimously not to take the risk of losing money, do not invest. Private equity investments are long term in nature.
Real names withheld

Summary of Key Points

Key Questions
1. What is an investment objective?
2. What is an investment philosophy?
3. How is an investment philosophy different from an investment strategy?
4. What is the investment management process?
5. What are the asset categories available?
6. How do we manage our investment portfolio?

Why do we need to establish investment philosophies and strategies?
A. Your investment club needs to establish investment philosophies to ensure you understand one another's core belief system and take that into consideration when making investment decisions.
B. Your investment philosophies become strategies you put into practice to guide every investment decision.
C. Your investment strategies should consider factors such as selected economic indices, political climate, risk tolerance levels, etc.

What Asset Classes Do We Consider?
A. An asset class is a group of investments that have similar characteristics, behave similarly, and are subject to similar market forces, laws, and regulations.
B. The four major asset classes defined in this book include equity, debt, cash, and alternative investments.
C. Seek expert advice on these asset classes before you make a final investment.

The investment Management Process

A. The investment management process requires adequate planning, execution, and monitoring for all investment decisions.
B. Allocate your club's funds based on your investment strategy and risk appetite.
C. Focus on building a balanced asset portfolio that will withstand economic cycles.

How Do We Manage Our Investment Portfolio?

A. Monitor and review your investment portfolio on a consistent basis.
B. Avoid making emotional decisions.
C. Outsource fund management if no one in the club has the time to manage and monitor funds.

Worksheet: Action Steps for Making Investment Decisions

Investment Philosophy

_____

_____

_____

_____

_____

Investment Strategy

_____

_____

_____

_____

_____

_____

_____

Asset Portfolio Mix (should add up to 100% and can be reviewed as appropriate)

Asset	% percentage range of Portfolio
e.g. Fixed Income Securities	20-40%

"Success in Investing
does not correlate with I.Q,
what you need is
the temperament to control
the urges that get other people
into trouble in investing."
- *Warren Buffett*

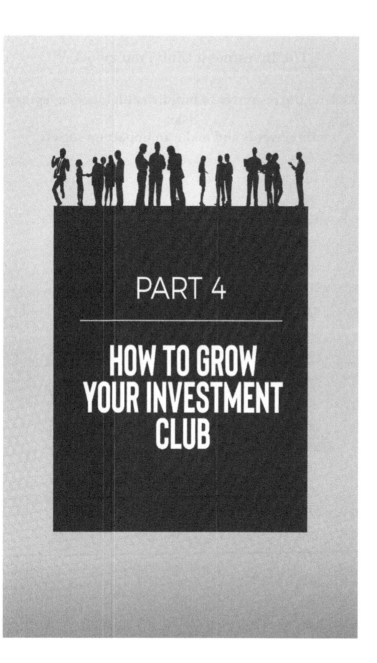

PART 4

HOW TO GROW YOUR INVESTMENT CLUB

The Investment Club Framework ™

Leveraging resources to build wealth together, spread risks,
gain rewards and make an impact on society.

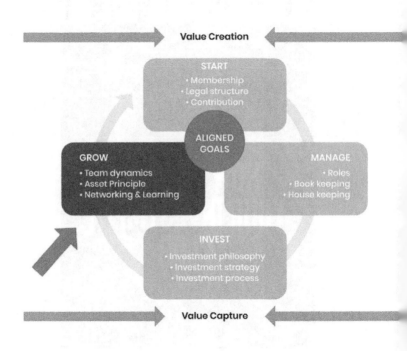

140

6
BUILD BRIDGES, NOT WALLS

"More bridges and fewer walls."
- *Tomie Balogun*

I stopped by at a local bookstore to get new books to read, per usual. While looking through the shelves, I heard a voice behind me say, "May I help you with anything?" I looked back and was intrigued to find a young girl. As we talked, she introduced me to her 10-year-old little sister — they were both interning at the bookstore. I had fun chatting with them about books, school, and why they decided to work during the holidays.

Finally, I asked what they were going to do with what they earned from the internship.

"Save it," the younger sister said with a huge smile.

"No, invest it and make more money," the older sister said.

I told her she was right on the money as that was what I would have done as well. Immediately, she asked if I would be interested in investing in her father's real estate company and proceeded to give me his phone number, so I could call and enquire about his company.

Yes, I did give her father a ring and had a great conversation with both parents. I told them they had amazing kids and they should be proud. Later that day, he emailed me an interesting proposal on investing in a real estate project. This incident taught me I could be presented with an investing opportunity by anyone, anywhere, even a child at a bookstore.

I have also received several investment opportunities simply from making conversation at events. For Nadia (in chapter 3), a good relationship with her bosses at work led to her discovering a great real estate opportunity that appreciated in value by 300%. She also had the right network of friends who were financially disciplined and willing to come together to take advantage of an investment opportunity.

It is essential to keep an open mind for investment opportunities. Of course, you should work within the set investment guidelines for your club but keep an open mind to learning about investment opportunities because you never know where you might stumble on such opportunities. Focus on fostering a
win/win relationship between your club and external parties. This will ensure that your investment club grows effectively over time.

Think Win/Win

Build a win/win environment within your investment club as well. One of the ways to do this is to manage one another's shortcomings with the
Asset Principle.[12] The asset principle replaces the popular accounting equation, **Assets + Liabilities = Equity** with the equation below:

Your Assets + Other People's Assets = Success

In the first equation, assets refer to your strengths, while liabilities refer to your weaknesses. Quite often, as individuals, we spend a lot of time trying to build our weaknesses into strengths. There is nothing wrong with that; however, the best your weaknesses may become will be weak strengths. Rather than spend all the time trying to build your weaknesses, focus instead on building your strengths and adding other people's strengths to the equation.

This is very important in an investment club. Your investment club is better off when every member contributes in an area of strength. Members are more likely to do their best and ensure the investment club succeeds.

How to Manage Club Dynamics

Kurt Lewin, a social psychologist and change management expert, is credited with coining the term "group dynamics" in the early 1940s. He noted that people often take on distinct roles and behaviors when they work in a group. "Group dynamics" describes the effects of these roles and behaviors on other group members, and on the group.

In an investment club, you can either have good dynamics or bad dynamics. A club with good dynamics consists of members who respect, trust, and hold one another accountable for growing the investment club sustainably.

Where you have bad dynamics, members of the club may find it difficult to agree on basic decisions, thus finding it difficult to get along.
Causes of bad dynamics include:

I. **Work Shedding** - When a few members do all the work while the others simply observe from a distance.

II. **Weak Leadership** - When the presiding member of the club makes decisions based on sentiments instead of clear facts.

III. **Different Goals and Objectives.**

To grow your investment club sustainably, use some of these principles to improve your club dynamics:

1) **Build a Diverse Team**

An investment club with members from different academic backgrounds, such as a mix of analytical thinkers and abstract thinkers (e.g. logical thinkers and visual artists), can significantly broaden a club's ability to tackle obstacles and grow successfully.13 One member of the club may be great at spotting the right opportunities in an industry or asset class, while another is great at negotiating the most favourable terms for a private investment.

2) **Identify a Leader Who Can Lead**

The quality of leadership may make or mar your investment club. A leader who considers all stake-holders and always seeks to unite the club is essential for the success and growth of your investment club. The leader needs to guide the growth of the club while also ensuring all stakeholder interests are managed.

When a team lacks a strong leader, a dominant member may take advantage of this and take charge. This often leads to disagreements and a lack of direction.

3) Define Roles and Responsibilities

All roles and responsibilities should be clearly defined and updated when required. Roles and responsibilities should be assigned based on indicated interest or on a need basis. Once roles and responsibilities are clearly defined, it will be easy for club members to understand their roles and how they all contribute to the successful growth of the investment club.

4) Focus on Communication

Take advantage of all open mediums to communicate freely with the members of your club. Communication mediums include group chat features on social media, conference calls, emails, and meetings.

Constant communication is vital for good group dynamics. Ensure all updates are communicated to all club members so that everyone has the same information. Open communication provides an opportunity for everyone to participate and contribute to the success of your investment club.

How to Originate Deals

Deal origination is the process of sourcing for investment prospects. An effective and efficient deal origination process results in successful investing.

Some of the ways to originate investment deals include:

1) **Network Effectively**
   Good networking is meeting the right people with the right prospects/influence. The right people can introduce your club to interesting investment opportunities you can take advantage of over time. It might not be immediate, but building the right relationships always pays off.

   Some interesting events where you may meet like-minded people include start-up pitch events, general enterprise fairs, and investment workshops/conferences. I am usually careful to check out information on past events (turn out, those who attended, etc.). This information helps me decide if an event is worth attending or not.

   Networking also refers to reaching out to friends within your network who might know of opportunities you can invest in as a club. While networking with friends you already know might help, the club should avoid making biased investment decisions due to an existing friendship. Always carry out due diligence and avoid making emotional decisions.

A great example of an event to network with like-minded individuals is the 'How to Invest' workshop, an event for young and experienced professionals who want to learn how to make better investment decisions.

2) **Leverage Social Media Platforms**
Social media provides the best of two worlds: a social presence and interaction with business prospects. One of the best ways to leverage social media is to build a presence on popular platforms such as Facebook, Twitter, LinkedIn, and various email lists.

A social presence provides a way for interested parties to connect with your investment club. It also gets you noticed by business owners with interesting business opportunities in the market place.

3) **Seek Investment Advisers**
Success, to a large extent, is determined by access to good advice when required. We had to learn this quite early in my investment club. We made several mistakes before we sought good advice that helped us navigate some volatile investment opportunities.

The best way to seek good advice is to seek out investment professionals who have a track record of transparent dealings, and request for a meeting. Work on making it a win/win relationship so it does not seem like you are taking undue advantage of their expertise.

Join Club 360 (the network of investment clubs in Africa).
It is free!

Club 360 is a network of investment clubs. It was established to provide support and leverage on investment opportunities amongst investment clubs across borders. In Club 360, we are focused on harnessing the power of all the clubs within our network to become a force to be reckoned with within our local and global economies. Some of the benefits of joining the investment club network include the following:

I.   Access to local and international investment opportunities shared by other clubs in the network.
II.   An opportunity to partner with other clubs (using an SPV) if your club lacks the required liquidity to invest in a particular project.
III. Access to a network of experts in various fields who can provide advice and insight that may protect you from fraud or loss of investment.
IV.   Discounted tickets to the various investor events.

To become a member of the network, you need to have an operational investment club and have started active contributions. Once you get started, visit www.tomiebalogun.com/club360 to join the network.

The Overthinking Trap

I will never forget the first experience I had with swimming. I signed up to take swimming lessons when it became clear that I was going to be the only member of my family sitting around the pool instead of diving in for a swim on a hot day.

My swimming instructor made us get into the pool to practice breathing underwater on the first day. I found the breathing exercises easy and looked forward to doing the glides. The pool was only 5 feet deep and I watched as others were trained and shown how to do the glides.
I saw them push themselves off the underwater wall, with arms stretched, glide towards the other end of the pool, and receive cheers from the instructor for making it to the end.

It looked easy enough from where I watched but when it came to my turn, I couldn't do it. I pushed off the wall but sputtered to a stop. I kept overthinking the actions I needed to take to glide successfully, and my safety guards went up. I had an intellectual understanding of all the actions I needed to take to carry out the glide successfully, but it was stuck in my mind. I couldn't bring my body to trust my mind and let go. After a couple of tries and almost giving up on my ability to swim, I did the glide. I arrived safely at the end of the pool, invigorated by my success in meeting this challenge.

That experience captures my final words for this book. This guide provides an intellectual understanding of all the actions you need to take to start, manage, and grow your investment club successfully, but don't get stuck with the details. Use the framework and adapt it to your club's ideals, vision, and peculiarities. Your investment club will work if your relationships work and if you are all flexible enough to think outside a box.

I wish I could say that once you make your investment club operational, a major part of your job is done. However, an investment club is a long-term effort. I hope you stick with it and it pays off for you.

Congratulations! You're on your way to starting your Investment Club. Now, some things to avoid and some things to note.

Here is a quick checklist of dos and don'ts:

Do	Do Not
1) Test and be willing to change your investment strategy over time.	1) Start an investment club with members who do not totally accept the club's wealth goal.
2) Keep proper financial records.	2) Contribute money and leave it in a savings account. Put the money to work by investing it.
3) Ensure everyone plays an active role in your investment club.	3) Start and operate an investment club without executing the necessary legal documents.
4) Build good dynamics within your club.	4) Make investment decisions based on sentiments. Don't invest in family or friends either.
5) Network effectively with other investment clubs and experts in the industry.	5) Encourage bad dynamics within your club.
6) Stay committed. It takes time.	6) Give up. Good things take time.

Summary of Key Points

Key Questions:
1) How do we grow our investment club?
2) How do we manage team dynamics?
3) How do we originate deals?

The Asset Principle
A. Build win/win relationships within your club and with external parties.
B. Manage one another's shortcomings with the asset principle. Focus on harnessing strengths and ignoring weaknesses.

How do we manage group dynamics?
A. Focus on building good dynamics in your club by respecting one another and holding one another accountable for the success of the club.
B. Avoid bad dynamics, which happens when members find it difficult to agree on basic decisions.
C. Some of the ways to avoid bad dynamics is to build a diverse team, identify a leader, define roles, and communicate effectively.

How do we originate deals?
A. Network effectively with the right people at the right events.
B. Build a social media presence on selected media platforms.
C. Seek experts who can provide professional advice.
D. Join the investment club network. It is free!

For further information on how to become licensed to teach a third party with my investment club framework, send an email to hello@tomiebalogun.com.

"When I work along
with two others,
from at least one I will
be able to learn."
- *Confucius*

Advice from Investment Clubs in Club 360

I think the greatest part of being a member of an investment club is being able to relax, understanding that I can reach out for help because I am not in this alone. Running investment ideas and financial decisions by the members of my club has blessed me with great feedback and insight. I do not feel scared anymore. Whatever I do not know, chances are my club mates do.

Start your investment club NOW and start with people who share similar values. Keep an open mind and be objective in decision-making. Sentiments can be dangerous. Rules are also very important. If you define your rules early, you can avoid making sentimental decisions. Finally, be legal. Laws protect.

- **D818 Club**

Start your investment club with friends who have similar investment or wealth goal(s). It makes setting investment goals and managing expectations easier. Secondly, be patient. It is a long and tedious journey. Don't expect instant gratification or glory. However, a clear objective and mindset from the start will assist greatly on your journey.

- **Midas Capital**

Don't be in a hurry. Start small (size of contribution and number of people allowed in the club). We have only 4 members in my club and setting up has been a task. Also, ensure that your goals are aligned. You don't want the club to be your growth bucket while another member sees it as a safety bucket. Finally, while waiting for your big investment break, invest in safe securities — mostly T-bills or anything that earns you interest while you're finalizing your investment policy.

- **Sekhel Capital**

The best part of being a member of an investment club is acting on investment opportunities and learning from actual experience. The discipline to stay committed to a long-term outlook and the knowledge that we are building wealth for the future also helps to keep us grounded.
Ensure your objectives are in alignment with the rest of the team and have an understanding that it will take a lot of discipline and patience. An investment club is not a get-rich-quick fix.

- **Keynes & Keys**

APPENDIX

(Sample guidelines for individual members of
a non-financial investment club)

Task 1- Start with your why

I recommend you start your accountability group with friends with whom you can be open, and who will be genuinely committed to seeing you achieve your goals and theirs.

Come up with a creative name for your group. A name that shows the pride you take in helping one another deliver on necessary goals. At the first meeting, each member of the group should individually take time to do tasks 2-4.

When each member is done with tasks 2-4, the other members should listen to that member share personal wealth goals and investment plan, while they offer words of advice or recommendations to help that member's plan.

Each member of the group should take turns to go through this process.

A Few Points to Note

A. The focus of an accountability group is to hold one another accountable to individual personal wealth goals.

B. When you invite people to join your group, describe its purpose clearly so everyone understands what is expected.

C. Keep the members of the group consistent and do not add new people all the time. You can seek a replacement if someone chooses to leave the group.

D. Kindly note that accountability groups may not work for everyone and that is ok. Give a gentle nudge if a member does not check in for a while, but do not push it.

E. Do not over complicate things. Keep your group simple and focused on the purpose.

F. Maintain a sense of humour. Don't take life too seriously. Hangout with one another and just have fun sometimes.

Task 2 - Identify your inflows and your outflows

One of the ways to prepare to invest is to save up cash to take advantage of investment opportunities when they come up.

The essential first step is to create an outline of your personal monthly inflow and personal monthly outflows. An inflow is personal income you earn or receive monthly

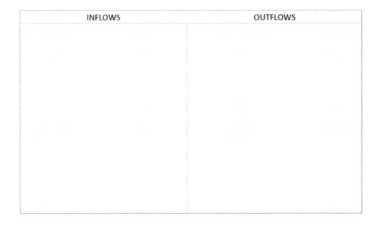

INFLOWS	OUTFLOWS

while an outflow is a personal expense or gift you make monthly.

Sum up your inflows and outflows. Deduct the sum of your outflows from the sum of your inflows.

A Few Points to Note

A. If the sum of your inflows exceeds the sum of your outflows, you are in a positive position. However, analyse each item of your outflows and check for where you are making excess or unnecessary expenses. Can you cut out the excesses or look for cheaper alternatives to some of your expenses? This will enable you to increase your positive position.

B. If your outflows exceed your inflows, you are in a negative position and something needs to be done immediately. What expenses can you stop making? What other sources of revenue can you start considering?

C. All personal outflows and inflows need to be separated from business outflows and inflows.

Task 3 -Set personal wealth goals and start a wealth creation fund

    A. If you are younger than 40, set a target net worth for when you are 40

    B. If you are older than 40, set a target net worth for when you are 50

Target net worth for when I'm 40/50

1) My target net worth when I'm 40/50 is :

_____

  (Fill in amount in currency of choice)

2) To achieve this goal, on a monthly basis I can set aside:

  (Fill in amount in currency of choice)

3) I plan to increase my monthly savings to

_____

  (Fill in amount in currency of choice)

By :   *(Set or make an estimate on a date)*

4) On an annual basis, that sums up to :

  (Multiply planned monthly savings by 12)

(Check to ensure your monthly savings plan can lead to your goal at 40/50 with or without any additional income)

Target savings for 20___ (Let's start now!)

1) How much money can I set aside, monthly in the year 20xx ? _____

(Fill in amount in currency of choice)
_____

2) At   the   end   of   20xx,   I   will   have
_____ *(Multiply planned monthly savings by 12)* in a savings account in preparation to make an investment in assets.

A Few Points to Note

A. Make a conscious decision to set aside cash for early investment. Automate the process so you can track progress.

B. Share your personal wealth goal with your friends for maximum impact. You might be afraid to share but you'll find that some of your friends will help you achieve your goals. Others will introduce to friends or resources that are helpful. You'll also find that your goals become clearer when you share.

Task 4 - Create an Investment plan

Identify assets for investment. Real estate is a great opportunity to build real wealth that appreciates over time.

Assets Categories	Worth
Cash/Cash equivalents	
Debt	
Stock (*Company shares*)	
Alternative investments	

(*Alternative investments are asset categories that are not cash equivalents, debt, or stock. It might be an investment in a specific project, commodities etc.*)

What steps are you going to take to make your investment plan happen?

1. _____

2. _____

3. _____

4. _____

5. _____

A Few Points to Note

A. Explore virgin investment opportunities to ensure you get real value from the assets in which you choose to invest.

B. Seek help from experts in different asset categories, such as an asset management company for assistance with securities, and a credible real estate firm for real estate purchases.

Task 5 - Commit to an accountability plan

The following outlines the steps to an accountability plan for each group:

1. All members of the group should commit to meeting regularly—weekly, monthly or quarterly. Group meetings should be conducted with everyone in attendance. The meetings can be conducted in person or using any of the social media group chats.

2. At meetings, members should share success stories (even if they are small) to create a bond and keep inspiration levels up.

3. Each meeting should end with a commitment by each member to action steps to be taken before the next meeting. Ensure the action steps are purposeful and not just task oriented.

4. At subsequent meetings, the group should start with reviewing action steps set for each member from the previous meetings and the results achieved.

5. Make a commitment to stretch yourselves to move forward towards accomplishing your goals, and even when there are setbacks, encourage and help one another. Allow constructive criticism and feedback with no ill feelings.

6. You can also share ideas, information, contacts, or resources during the meetings or anytime you use a social media group chat.

7. Finally, end on a note of gratitude for the group—all you have   achieved and will achieve together.

A Few Points to Note

A. The real value of the group is accountability—when you and members of your group hold one another accountable to your personal wealth goals and plans. People are more productive when they have a deadline and are held accountable to it.

B. The key to a successful accountability group is to all be invested in each member's personal wealth goals. Collaboration beats competition any day.

[1] *some of the notes on this page are culled from the book 'The Success Principles' by Jack Canfield.*

About the Author

Tomie Balogun is on a mission to teach working professionals how to take advantage of the power of many and start investment clubs. As a result, she is considered a leading expert on how to start, manage and grow investment clubs in Nigeria.

Her working career spans three industries: management consulting, telecommunications, and more recently, financial technology.

In a bid to be deliberate about her finances, she co-founded Midas Capital (which started out as an investment club until it formalized) in 2013 and so far, the company has invested in three (3) start-up businesses; a transportation company, an e-commerce company, Domestico.ng, in Nigeria, and a palm oil processing company, Tabriss Ltd.

Prior to this, she was on an accelerated International Leadership Program in Bharti Airtel for selected young African leaders who showed immense promise. The leadership program culminated in a role as a business planning and budget analyst in Airtel Nigeria Limited. Tomie also had a stint with the International Financial Corporation (IFC), an arm of the World Bank, as a consultant advising on projects within the manufacturing and agribusiness sectors in Nigeria.

In addition to building awareness on investment clubs, Tomie works with financial technology (Fintech) organizations as a product design and development specialist. In her work with Fintech organizations, she examines opportunities for growth with a focus on technology's impact on scale, value, and financial inclusion. She gained product design and development experience while leading a strategic business unit in Greystone Partners Limited.

Tomie holds a bachelor's degree in Economics and is an MBA graduate of the prestigious Lagos Business School (LBS). She serves as a Director on the board of three (3) SME's in Nigeria; Midas Capital Ltd, Velocity Logistics Ltd, and Salami's Equity Ltd.

NOTES

Chapter 1 -Gaining Clarity

1. Lagos Business School (LBS). Lagos Business School is the graduate business school of the Pan-Atlantic University, Nigeria. LBS offers academic programs in management that have been ranked among the best in Africa. LBS is a member of the Association of African Business Schools (AABS), the Global Business School Network (GBSN), and Association to Advance Collegiate Schools of Business (AACSB International).
2. *Ajo* or *Esusu* are traditional savings schemes in the informal and formal sectors of the economy.
3. The How to Invest Workshop is an annual workshop organized for young professionals and entrepreneurs who want to learn how to make better investment decisions. The workshop typically features panels of experts who break down the complex investment world.
4. My personal website is www.tomiebalogun.com. My free e-book, *'5 Steps to Breaking Average'*, can be downloaded at www.tomiebalogun.com/start/
5. Inflation rate. https://tradingeconomics.com/united-states/inflation-cpi

6. World Inflation rate.
https://www.indexmundi.com/world/inflation_rate
_(consumer_prices).html
7. Nigeria Inflation rate.
https://tradingeconomics.com/nigeria/inflation-cpi
8. How did Warren Buffet build his fortune?
http://theconservativeincomeinvestor.com/2014/01/
26/how-did-warren-buffett-build-his-fortune/

Chapter 2- Breaking Average

1. Better Investing Educational Series. *Investment Club Operations Handbook* – sample chapter [online] Available at
http://www.Betterinvesting.Org/Investing/Landing/Investmentclubstarter/Resources/FREE_ICOH_Chapter.Pdf
2. Better Investing Educational Series. *Investment Club Operations Handbook* – sample chapter [online], Available at
http://www.Betterinvesting.Org/Investing/Landing/Investmentclubstarter/Resources/FREE_ICOH_Chapter.Pdf
3. The Sage of Madison Heights [online] Available at https://expectingalpha.com/2016/05/17/the-sage-of-madison-heights/
4. Investments (1971) Limited; Story of a model, Investment practice and prospects in Nigeria, A

commemorative publication of Investments (1971) limited, Lagos

5. Central Bank of Nigeria (CBN), 2013, Monthly average exchange rates of the Naira (Naira per unit of foreign currency) [online] Available at https://www.cbn.gov.ng/rates/exrate.asp?year=201 3

Chapter 3 - The Art of the Start

1. Limited Partnership. At the time of publishing this book, Lagos State is the only state in Nigeria that has adopted the LLP business structure and there are reservations about the applicability and recognition or otherwise for LLPs not registered in Lagos State
2. General Partnership Tax Advantage. https://www.wrighthassall.co.uk/knowledge/legal-articles/2011/02/20/key-characteristics-limited-liability-partnerships/
3. Co-operative Society Tax Exemption. http://www.oseroghoassociates.com/component/content/article?id=14&print=1&download=0

Chapter 4- Group Effort, Not Individual Effort

1. Bivio, Sample Investment Club Operating Procedures, [online], Available at https://Www.Bivio.Com/Site-Help/Bp/Sample_Operating_Procedures. [Accessed 14 Jan 2017]

Chapter 4- This Is What We Came to Do

1   Aswath Damodaran, A.S, (2007). *Investment Philosophy: The secret ingredient in investment success.* [online] Available at http://People.Stern.Nyu.Edu/Adamodar/Pdfiles/In vphiloh/Invhalfday2007.Pdf

2   Aswath Damodaran, A.S, (2007). *Investment Philosophy: The secret ingredient in investment success.* [online] Available at http://People.Stern.Nyu.Edu/Adamodar/Pdfiles/In vphiloh/Invhalfday2007.Pdf

3   Aswath Damodaran, A.S, (2007). *Investment Philosophy: The Secret Ingredient in Investment Success.* [online] Available at http://People.Stern.Nyu.Edu/Adamodar/Pdfiles/In vphiloh/Invhalfday2007.Pdf

4   Brian Boyer, B.B, (2011). *The Case for Alternative Investments in a Diversified Portfolio.* [online] Available at https://www.wespath.com/assets/1/7/4323.pdf

5   Brian Boyer, B.B, (2011). *The Case for Alternative Investments in a Diversified Portfolio.* [online] Available at https://www.wespath.com/assets/1/7/4323.pdf

6   T. Rowe Price Investment services. *Managing Your Investment Portfolio.* [online] Available at https://individual.troweprice.com/public/Retail/Pla nning-&-Research/Investing-101/Manage-Your-Portfolio

Chapter 5 - Build Bridges, Not Walls

1. The asset principle. Heard it for the first time at a TFD series with Mrs. Ibukun Awosika, Chairperson, First Bank Nigeria Plc.
2. Christopher Cascio. *What Are Some of the Advantages of Diversity in Teams?* [online] Available at http://classroom.synonym.com/advantages-diversity-teams-7494.html

Made in the USA
Las Vegas, NV
13 July 2024